Moral Fictionalism

Lines of Thought

Short philosophical books

General editors: Peter Ludlow and Scott Sturgeon
Published in association with the Aristotelian Society

Moral Fictionalism

Mark Eli Kalderon

CLARENDON PRESS · OXFORD

OXFORD
UNIVERSITY PRESS

Great Clarendon Street, Oxford OX2 6DP

Oxford University Press is a department of the University of Oxford.
If furthers the University's objective of excellence in research, scholarship,
and education by publishing worldwide in

Oxford New York

Auckland Cape Town Dar es Salaam Hong Kong Karachi
Kuala Lumpur Madrid Melbourne Mexico City Nairobi
New Delhi Shanghai Taipei Toronto

With offices in

Argentina Austria Brazil Chile Czech Republic France Greece
Guatemala Hungary Italy Japan South Korea Poland Portugal
Singapore Switzerland Thailand Turkey Ukraine Vietnam

Published in the United States
by Oxford University Press Inc., New York
© Mark Eli Kalderon 2005
The moral rights of the author have been asserted
Database right Oxford University Press (maker)

First published 2005

British Library Cataloguing in Publication Data
Data available

Library of Congress Cataloging in Publication Data
Data available
ISBN 0-19-927597-1 9780199275977

1 3 5 7 9 10 8 6 4 2

Typeset by Kolam Information Services Pvt. Ltd, Pondicherry, India
Printed in Great Britain on acid-free paper by
Biddles Ltd, King's Lynn, Norfolk

In memory of my father,
Dr Albert Eli Kalderon

One cannot give too many or too frequent warnings against this laxity, or even mean cast of mind, which seeks its principle among empirical motives and laws; for, human reason in its weariness gladly rests on this pillow and in a dream of sweet illusions (which allow it to embrace a cloud instead of Juno) it substitutes for morality a bastard patched up from limbs of quite diverse ancestry, which looks like whatever one wants to see in it but not like virtue for him who has once seen virtue in her true form.

Kant (1785: 4: 426)

PREFACE

MORAL realists maintain that morality has a distinctive subject matter. Specifically, realists maintain that moral discourse is representational, that moral sentences express moral propositions—propositions that attribute moral properties to things. Noncognitivists, in contrast, standardly maintain that the realist imagery associated with morality is a fiction, a reification of our noncognitive attitudes. The thought that there is a distinctively moral subject matter is regarded as something to be debunked by philosophical reflection on the way moral discourse mediates and makes public our noncognitive attitudes (hence the familiar deployment of the Humean metaphor of projection). The realist fiction might be understood as a philosophical misconception of a discourse that is not fundamentally representational but whose intent is rather practical. There is, however, another way to understand the realist fiction. Perhaps the subject matter of morality is a fiction that stands in no need of debunking but is rather the means by which our attitudes are conveyed. Perhaps moral sentences express moral propositions, just as the realist maintains, but in uttering a moral sentence competent speakers do not assert the moral proposition expressed but rather convey by means of it the relevant noncognitive attitudes. Thus, in calling abortion wrong, Bernice conveys, say, her disapproval of abortion and does so by invoking a fiction in which acts of abortion instantiate the property of wrongness. Bernice utters a sentence that expresses the proposition that abortion is wrong, but she does not assert that proposition but rather conveys by means of it her disapproval of abortion.

Noncognitivism, in its primary sense, is a claim about moral acceptance: the acceptance of a moral sentence is not belief in a moral proposition but is some other attitude. Standardly, noncognitivism has been linked to nonfactualism—the claim that moral content is nonrepresentational, that the content of a moral sentence does not consist in its expressing a moral proposition but rather consists in its nonrepresentational role in moral discourse. Specifically, the content of a moral sentence is said instead to consist in its conveying the noncognitive attitude involved in its acceptance. Indeed, the terms 'noncognitivism' and 'nonfactualism' have been used interchangeably. But this misses an important possibility; for moral content may be representational, but the acceptance of moral sentences might not be belief in the moral proposition expressed, and its utterance might not be the assertion of that proposition. This possibility constitutes a novel form of noncognitivism, *moral fictionalism*. Whereas nonfactualists seek to debunk the realist fiction of a moral subject matter, the moral fictionalist claims that that fiction stands in no need of debunking but is the means by which the noncognitive attitudes involved in moral acceptance are conveyed by moral utterance. So there are two varieties of noncognitivism: nonfactualism and fictionalism. Moral fictionalism is noncognitivism without a nonrepresentational semantics.

The central aim of this study is to articulate in sufficiently general terms what moral fictionalism is, how it differs from the usual alternatives to moral realism, and what can be said in favor of it. Special attention will be given to nonfactualism since nonfactualism and fictionalism are each forms of noncognitivism.

The present study began when I was teaching at UCLA. While rereading *After Virtue*, Alasdair MacIntyre's claim that, even if emotivism provided the wrong account of the meaning of moral sentences, it might still provide the right account of their use struck me with the force of revelation. I realized that this was the germ of a novel form of moral irrealism, distinct from both nonfactualism and the error theory. I tried to write a paper. No one understood it. Discussing the matter with my readers, it became clear that the topic required an extended treatment. Without meaning to, I ended up writing this book.

I would like to thank the participants of three seminars I gave at UCL where versions of this material were presented. I would also like to thank the participants of a UCL faculty colloquium, the participants of the Birkbeck philosophy study weekend at Cumberland Lodge, and the participants of an Oxford Moral Seminar Series where material from Chapter 1 was presented, as well as the participants of a one-day conference on moral fictionalism sponsored by the Philosophy Programme of the School for Advanced Study at the University of London, where material from Chapter 2 was presented. Thanks to Scott Soames, who read an early treatment of this subject matter and encouraged me to develop it further. Thanks to James Dreier, M. G. F. Martin, Veroniqué Munoz-Dardé, Gideon Rosen, Maja Spener, Thomas Smith, Scott Sturgeon, Ralph Wedgwood, and José Zalabardo, all of whom read at least portions of the manuscript, some of whom read the entire manuscript, and each of whom gave invaluable advice.

The contributions of two people were indispensable early on. Michael Thau kindly read the original paper of which this book is a descendant. If it were not for his patient and generous comments on that paper this book would not exist. Discussion and correspondence with Mark van Roojen were both instructive and a great source of encouragement. Thanks to both. Neither is, of course, to blame for what I have made of their input.

The book was completed while on leave from UCL. Thanks are due both to UCL and to my Head of Department, Jo Wolff, who was instrumental in securing a sabbatical for me. This research was partially supported by the Arts and Humanities Research Board under their Extended Leave Scheme.

M.E.K.

London

CONTENTS

I

Moral Pyrrhonism and Noncognitivism

Introduction

WHAT is the nature of moral commitment?

Cognitivists claim that a person's moral commitments consist, at least in part, in their moral beliefs. So if Edgar is a moral vegetarian, then Edgar believes that it is wrong to kill animals for food. After all, we regularly describe our moral commitments as moral beliefs, and thus it is plausible that we hold such beliefs when we are so committed. Notice that Edgar's belief that it is wrong to kill animals for food is a moral belief, a belief with a moral proposition as its object. A morally committed person may hold moral beliefs, but that is not to say that a person's moral commitments involve no attitudes other than moral belief. So, for example, a cognitivist could concede that, in being a moral vegetarian, Edgar is averse to killing animals for food, where Edgar's aversion is a noncognitive attitude. Indeed, a cognitivist might plausibly claim that Edgar is averse to eating animals for food because he believes that it is wrong, and that Edgar's aversion is only an aspect of his moral commitment insofar as there are moral grounds for it. Cognitivists need not deny that moral commitments involve noncognitive attitudes; cognitivists claim only that moral beliefs are indispensable to explaining a person's moral commitments.

In contrast, noncognitivists claim that a person's moral commitments are best explained by attitudes other than moral belief. While we may describe our moral commitments in terms of the moral beliefs we hold, the sense in which we hold such beliefs is best explained in terms of our noncognitive attitudes. Moral beliefs may be dispensable to explaining moral commitment, but that is not to say that a person's moral commitments involve no belief. So, for example, a noncognitivist could concede that, in being committed to the claim that it was wrong of her to lie to Edgar, Bernice believes that she lied to Edgar. It is just that this belief is not a moral belief. Bernice may believe, but Bernice believes no distinctively moral proposition. Noncognitivists need not deny that moral commitments involve cognitive attitudes; noncognitivists claim only that a person's moral commitments are best explained by attitudes other than belief in a moral proposition.

So cognitivists claim that a person's moral commitments are best explained by the moral beliefs he holds while noncognitivists claim that a person's moral commitments are best explained by attitudes other than moral belief. This difference is partly a difference in the nature of the attitudes involved in moral commitment (whether they are cognitive or noncognitive) and partly a difference in the content of these attitudes (whether the cognitive attitudes involved, if any, have moral propositions as their objects). This explanatory difference, however, is a manifestation of a more fundamental normative difference. Cognitivists and noncognitivists fundamentally differ about the norms governing moral commitment: Whereas cognitivists maintain that they are appropriate to belief in a moral proposition, noncognitivists deny this, emphasizing instead the nonrepresentational function of moral commitment. (That the difference is fundamentally normative is substantiated by the argument of the section *Relativity and Error*.)

Acceptance

In this dispute between cognitivists and noncognitivists, how are we to determine the nature and content of the attitudes involved in moral commitment?

Moral commitments are expressed by moral sentences and incurred by competent speakers accepting moral sentences. As this linguistic observation is common ground between the cognitivist and the noncognitivist, one might begin with it and see if moral commitment can be neutrally characterized in terms of what a competent speaker is committed to in accepting a moral sentence. The idea is that one might then determine, in a non-question-begging manner, the nature and content of the attitudes involved in moral commitment, by determining the nature and content of the attitudes involved in accepting a moral sentence. 'Acceptance' here is a technical term and is explicitly stipulated to be neutral between cognitivist and noncognitivist understandings of the commitment incurred. It is useful to have a neutral term in order to pose the question whether the acceptance of a sentence in a given area is best understood as belief in the proposition expressed or as some other attitude. (Here I am following van Fraassen's, 1980, usage.) The rationale for the procedure is twofold: First, the content of the accepted moral sentence is evidence about the contents of the relevant attitudes, since it plausibly constrains the contents of the attitudes involved in accepting that sentence. Second, the functional role of moral acceptance, the role that moral acceptance plays in moral discourse and in the cognitive psychology of competent speakers, is evidence about the nature of the relevant attitudes. Given this terminology, the dispute between the cognitivist and the noncognitivist becomes the following: given the norms governing moral acceptance, is the acceptance of a moral sentence belief in a moral proposition expressed?

Acceptance is best understood in terms of its role in inquiry. Inquiry is not a solitary activity, at least not primarily. All successful forms of inquiry, such as physics, economics, literary theory, and so on, are *public* endeavors. Since successful forms of inquiry are public endeavors, their results are nonaccidentally presented in the medium of public language. Thus, for example, biology is a domain of inquiry, and associated with it is a region of discourse that involves a class of public language sentences couched in the distinctive vocabulary of that discipline. Morality itself constitutes a public domain of inquiry, albeit a distinctively practical one. When a person deliberates about his obligations to others, he inquires about his obligations to others and so engages in moral inquiry. Given the point of a person's deliberating about his obligations to others, it is nonaccidental that the results of such deliberation—and, indeed, the deliberation itself—can be presented in the medium of public language. Thus, associated with moral inquiry is a region of discourse that involves a class of public language sentences couched in a distinctive vocabulary. For the sake of simplicity, I will assume throughout that moral vocabulary consists solely in a class of moral predicates (such as 'good' and 'just'). This is a deliberate idealization: moral vocabulary also includes substantives (such as 'goodness' and 'justice') and, arguably at least, modal auxiliaries (such as 'must'). However, these important grammatical distinctions will be irrelevant to what follows.

The sentences of at least some regions of discourse express propositions relative to a context of utterance. Normally, the proposition expressed by a sentence is what is conveyed, among other things, in uttering that sentence in that context. Propositions are the primary bearers of truth and falsity. Sentences may be evaluated as true or false, but they inherit their truth-value from the proposition they express in the context of utterance. Moreover, propositions are the objects of attitudes such as belief and assertion. This is not, of course, to claim that all attitudes are propositional. Edgar may be averse to eating meat, but the object of that attitude is not a proposition. I was careful to say that the sentences of *some* regions of discourse express propositions. Perhaps in other regions of discourse sentences fail to express propositions, but rather have a nonrepresentational content. So, while the sentences of at least some regions of discourse express propositions relative to a context of utterance, I will not assume that the sentences of every region of discourse are representational in the sense of expressing propositions that represent the putative subject matter of the given domain of inquiry.

We are assuming that moral vocabulary consists solely in a class of moral predicates. If moral predicates denote moral properties, then sentences that contain moral predicates express moral propositions—propositions that attribute moral properties to things. So conceived, the subject matter of moral inquiry would be the existence and distribution of moral properties. It is in this sense that we will understand the cognitivist's claim that the norms governing moral acceptance are appropriate to belief in the *moral* proposition expressed by the accepted moral sentence, and it is in this sense that we will understand the noncognitivist's denial. Instead, standard noncognitivists maintain that moral predicates do not denote moral properties, and hence that the sentences that contain them fail to express moral propositions; rather, moral predicates play a nonrepresentational role in moral discourse, and hence have a nonrepresentational content.

Public inquiry involves the production and the use of sentences from the associated region of discourse. There are two aspects of acceptance corresponding to these two features of public inquiry. Accepting a sentence from the region of discourse is both the object of inquiry and its grounds. Acceptance is the object of inquiry in the sense that it is a state that represents the end of inquiry: in accepting a sentence, a person no longer takes himself to have a reason to investigate further, to continue to inquire whether or not to accept that sentence. Moreover, a person is justified in accepting a sentence if he possesses sufficient reason to inquire no further. Not only is acceptance the object of inquiry, but it is also the grounds of inquiry: in accepting a sentence S, not only does a person no longer take himself to have a reason to continue to inquire about S, but he also relies on his acceptance of S as grounds for further theoretical and practical inquiry. Acceptance is the grounds of inquiry in the sense that a person relies on the acceptance of the sentence in theoretical and practical reasoning and takes himself to be justified in so doing. These two aspects of acceptance are related: a person could be said to accept a sentence only if he was prepared to rely on it in theoretical and practical reasoning over a wide range of contexts. Moreover, a person would be justified in relying on S in theoretical and practical reasoning if he were justified in accepting S, if he had sufficient reason to inquire no further.

Acceptance is governed by norms and so is subject to criticism. Some of these norms are internal to the domain of inquiry; others are external to it. In a certain cultural and historical context, the acceptance of heliocentric astronomy may be criticized as impious, at least by one relevant norm or standard of impiety. However, the acceptance of heliocentric astronomy is not bad astronomy. The charge of impiety is not an astronomical criticism and relies on norms external to astronomical inquiry. Given the norms internal to astronomical inquiry, the acceptance of a heliocentric astronomy is not subject to criticism. Of course, being acceptable by internal norms need not guarantee genuine acceptability. The claim that Mercury rising has an unsettling effect on a person's psychology might be acceptable, if it is, by the norms of acceptance internal to astrology, but it is not acceptable by external norms that many of us accept and regard as authoritative.

Acceptance can be tentative or full (see Harman, 1986: 46–7). A person tentatively accepts a claim when, for example, he accepts a hypothesis in order to work out its implications. Thus, for example, while Edgar denies the axiom of choice, he might nevertheless tentatively accept that axiom in order to work out the implications of conjoining it with a standard set theory. Though Edgar tentatively accepts the axiom of choice, he does not fully accept it given his explicit denial. Notice that Edgar has a reason to accept the axiom of choice only while he has a reason to inquire after its implications for a standard set theory. Once he discovers some relevant set of implications, inquiry ends and there is no further need to accept the axiom. Tentative acceptance is not limited to supposition. To see this consider the following. Bernice only tentatively accepts General Relativity. Her acceptance of General Relativity is less than full acceptance in the sense that she is self-consciously prepared to give it up: she regards General Relativity as a very good approximation of the truth but an imperfect approximation nonetheless. Bernice has reason to accept General Relativity only while there is no significantly more accurate alternative. Tentative acceptance, while distinct from full acceptance, is a matter of degree. The degree of tentative acceptance depends on the extent to which a person relies on the acceptance of a sentence in theoretical and practical reasoning and the range of contexts in which a person does so rely. Thus, Bernice's tentative acceptance of General Relativity is significantly more extensive than Edgar's tentative acceptance of the axiom of choice. If, over time, and over a wide range of contexts, a person comes to rely sufficiently on the acceptance of a sentence in theoretical and practical reasoning, he may come to fully accept that sentence. Thus, the distinction between tentative and full acceptance is best understood as an approach to a limit.

In contrast to tentative acceptance, full acceptance ends inquiry. In fully accepting a sentence, the issue is closed, in the sense that there is no reason to inquire further. A person is justified in fully accepting a sentence if, by the norms internal to inquiry or by authoritative norms external to it, he possesses sufficient reason to end inquiry. At issue in debate between cognitivists and noncognitivists is the nature and content of the attitudes involved in the full acceptance of moral sentences, and so only the norms governing full moral acceptance are relevant. To see this, consider the following. Bernice only tentatively accepts General Relativity. Suppose that her tentative acceptance falls short of belief. This would not establish that scientific acceptance consists wholly in attitudes other than belief in the accepted theory. Similarly, suppose that Edgar only tentatively accepts that it is wrong to kill animals for food. Suppose, moreover, that his tentative acceptance falls short of belief. This would not establish that moral acceptance consists wholly in attitudes other than belief in a moral proposition. It is the nature and content of the attitudes involved in the full acceptance of a moral sentence that is at issue in the debate between cognitivists and noncognitivists. While cognitivists maintain that full moral acceptance involves belief in the moral proposition expressed by the accepted moral sentence, noncognitivists deny this. Thus, only the norms governing full moral acceptance are relevant to determining the cognitive status of moral commitment. Henceforth, by 'acceptance' I will mean full acceptance.

The Argument from Intransigence

Why think that moral acceptance is noncognitive?

According to familiar internalist arguments for noncognitivism, there is a *motivational* difference between moral acceptance and belief: accepting a moral sentence motivates a person to act in a way that belief does not. I will not argue in this way for noncognitivism; rather, I will argue that there is an *epistemic* difference between moral acceptance and belief. I will not argue that moral acceptance has a motivational property that belief lacks; rather, I will argue that belief has an epistemic property that moral acceptance lacks. This epistemic difference is brought out by the commitments incurred by reasonable and interested people engaged in a certain kind of disagreement, what Scanlon (1995) describes as a 'disagreement about reasons.' In cognitive inquiry, under certain conditions, people engaged in a disagreement about reasons have a motive that, in moral inquiry, under similar conditions, they would lack. This could only be so if moral acceptance were noncognitive. Or so I will argue.

Disagreements about Reasons

Suppose that Edgar and Bernice disagree about some sentence S. While Edgar accepts S, Bernice rejects S. Though she rejects S, Bernice strikes Edgar as an otherwise rational and reasonable human being—she can at least think and talk as well as Edgar. The mere fact of disagreement need not bother Edgar, for he might plausibly think that their disagreement derives from Bernice's ignorance of the relevant evidence. Suppose, however, that Edgar engages Bernice in discussion and rules out this possibility: Edgar and Bernice share a common body of evidence. Not only is Bernice fully informed about the evidence that Edgar accepts, but she is also internally coherent in taking that evidence as a reason for rejecting S—just as Edgar is internally coherent in taking that evidence as a reason for accepting S. While they share a common body of evidence, they nonetheless disagree about its epistemic significance and are internally coherent in doing so. Given that each is internally coherent, each can offer what the other would regard as a question-begging argument for their acceptance or rejection of S. So both are otherwise rational and reasonable, fully informed, and can offer what the other would regard as a question-begging argument for their acceptance or rejection of S.

Edgar and Bernice's positions conflict: they disagree about whether to accept or reject S. However, if we focus solely on the fact of conflict, we will miss something important about their disagreement. For Edgar and Bernice disagree not only about which sentence to accept in the given circumstance, they apparently disagree about what would count as a reason for acceptance in the given circumstance. Edgar and Bernice disagree about the norms governing acceptance: they implicitly accept distinct principles that determine what would count as a reason for acceptance in the given circumstance. This is manifest in a phenomenological difference between them. From Edgar's perspective, certain features of their circumstances are salient and have a certain normative appearance—they seem to be reasons for accepting S. From Bernice's perspective, potentially distinct features of their circumstances are salient and have a different normative appearance—they seem to be reasons for rejecting S. The world, as they commonly understand it, differs in the normative appearance it presents to each. Since Edgar and Bernice disagree not only about S but also what would count as a reason for accepting or rejecting S, their disagreement is a disagreement about reasons.

To get a better sense of this, consider how the traditional problem of induction can be recast as a disagreement about reasons. Suppose that Edgar is an inductivist: he believes that the regularities manifest in his experience are representative of the regularities that obtain in nature generally, even in the unobserved portions of nature. Suppose Edgar discovers that other people with distinct scientific traditions and cultures disagree with him. Bernice, for example, is a counterinductivist. Far from accepting the uniformity of nature, Bernice's beliefs about the unobservable are guided by a different principle, the non-uniformity of nature: Bernice believes that her experience is positively misleading in the sense that an observed regularity is evidence that it does not obtain in nature generally—indeed, that it will fail in the very next instance. Though she denies the uniformity of nature, Bernice strikes Edgar as an otherwise rational and reasonable human being—she can at least think and talk as well as Edgar. The mere fact of disagreement need not bother Edgar, for he might plausibly think their disagreement derives from Bernice's ignorance of the relevant evidence. Bernice might have been raised in an idiosyncratic, environmental niche where observed regularities are an unreliable guide to the regularities that obtain more generally in that environment, or she might have somehow failed to reflect adequately on what must have been a track record of predictive failure. Suppose, however, that Edgar engages Bernice in conversation and rules out these possibilities. It seems possible that Edgar may come, over time, to think that, just as his acceptance of the uniformity of nature is coherent given all the evidence, so is Bernice's acceptance of the nonuniformity of nature. So both are otherwise rational and reasonable, fully informed, and can offer what the other would regard as a question-begging argument for their epistemic positions.

When Edgar and Bernice disagree about some theoretical sentence S, their epistemic positions conflict: they disagree about whether to accept or reject S. However, if we focus solely on the fact of conflict, we will miss something important about their disagreement. For Edgar and Bernice disagree not only about which sentence to accept in the given circumstance, they apparently disagree about what would count as a reason for acceptance in the given circumstance. Edgar accepts a principle according to which observable regularities count as a reason to accept that such regularities obtain in nature more generally, even in the unobserved parts of nature. Bernice, in contrast, accepts a principle according to which observable regularities count as a reason to *reject* that such regularities obtain in nature more generally. So Edgar and Bernice not only disagree about S, they implicitly accept distinct principles that determine what would count as a reason for acceptance. This is manifest in a phenomenological difference between them. From Edgar's perspective, observable regularities are salient and appear to be a reason for believing that they obtain in nature more generally. From Bernice's perspective, observable regularities are salient and appear to be a reason for believing that they do not obtain in nature more generally. Since Edgar and Bernice disagree not only about S but also about what would count as a reason for accepting or rejecting S, their disagreement is a disagreement about reasons.

The disagreements described above, where the participants are otherwise rational and reasonable, fully informed, and can offer what the other would regard as a question-begging argument for their acceptance or rejection of S, are highly idealized. Indeed, so described, no such disagreements ever occur. No two people ever share precisely the same information, and it is impossible to say in advance of inquiry what information will be relevant to the acceptance or rejection of S. So no actual disagreement involves full information in the way described. These idealized cases of disagreement are nonetheless useful in dramatizing what is at issue in disagreement about reasons. What is at issue is not only whether to accept or reject S, but what would count as a reason to accept or reject S. What is at issue is the correct relevant principle that determines what counts as a reason for accepting or rejecting S in the given circumstance:

> *Disagreement about Reasons*
> In a disagreement about reasons, the disputants not only disagree about whether to accept or reject some sentence S, they disagree about what would count as a reason to accept or reject S in the given circumstance. Specifically, in a disagreement about reasons, the disputants, at least impli-

citly, accept distinct principles that count potentially distinct features of the circumstance as reasons for the acceptance or rejection of S.

Disagreements about reasons, however, need not occur in so idealized a form. So, for example, otherwise rational and reasonable palaeontologists can agree about the fossil record and yet disagree about what that record establishes. If they do, they are engaged in a disagreement about reasons: each implicitly accepts distinct principles that count potentially distinct aspects of the fossil record as reasons for the acceptance or rejection of the target claim. Similarly, constructivists and classical mathematicians disagree about what counts as a reason for accepting a mathematical sentence. Not only are methodological disputes in the special sciences disagreements about reasons, but so are disagreements that result from different styles of inductive reasoning. Disagreements about reasons may be theoretical, but they can be practical as well. Thus, Scanlon writes:

[Disagreement about reasons] is surely possible and perhaps even common. I think that it is plausible to suggest that we have an example of it in the contemporary disagreement between secular liberals like me, who see nothing morally objectionable about homosexuality, and conservative Christians who believe that it is a serious wrong. (Scanlon 1995: 352)

While in their idealized form disagreements about reasons plausibly never occur, in less idealized form such disagreements are plausibly ubiquitous.

Reacting to Disagreement

What is the rational response to a disagreement about reasons?

If we confine ourselves to what can be deontically described, then not only is it rationally permissible for Edgar to persist in his acceptance of S, but it is also rationally permissible for Edgar to revise—to reject or suspend judgment concerning S.

Edgar's persistence in his acceptance of S might be rationally permissible on a number of grounds. So, for example, in a cognitive domain Edgar might persist in his acceptance of S, despite the disagreement about reasons, on the grounds of doxastic conservativism. Doxastic conservativism is the epistemic policy of persisting in one's beliefs unless presented with a positive reason to change one's mind (see Harman, 1986: chapter 4). Since the evidence's having a different normative appearance for Bernice is not a positive reason for Edgar to change his mind, if doxastic conservativism is a genuine epistemic norm, then it is rationally permissible for Edgar to persist in his belief that S.

Doxastic conservativism is not the only grounds for the rational permissibility of persistence. Suppose, owing to some psychological necessity, Edgar simply cannot give up his acceptance of S. Since he must accept S, and is not self-contradictory or otherwise internally incoherent in so doing, it might be rationally permissible for him to persist in his acceptance of S.

Just as it is rationally permissible for Edgar to persist in his acceptance of S, it is rationally permissible for him to revise—to reject or suspend judgment concerning S. Revision might be rationally permissible on a number of grounds. So, for example, it might be rationally permissible for Edgar to revise if, upon reflection, he came to accept a debunking explanation for the disagreement between himself and Bernice, i.e. if he came to explain their disagreement in terms accidentally connected to reasons for acceptance. (See Cohen's, 2000, discussion of the paradox of conviction.)

Coming to accept a debunking explanation is not the only grounds for the rational permissibility of revision. Suppose that Edgar came to believe that there is a perfect symmetry between his epistemic position and Bernice's. Edgar could not coherently be a cognitivist and persist in accepting S, and in accepting that Bernice is wrong in rejecting S, while maintaining that there is a perfect epistemic symmetry between them. (See Rosen's, 2001, discussion of the dispute between realists and fictionalists about abstracta.) If reflection on the disagreement about reasons prompts Edgar to accept a debunking explanation of their disagreement, or to accept that there is a perfect epistemic symmetry between himself and Bernice, then it would be rationally permissible for Edgar to revise—to reject or suspend judgment concerning S.

If we confine ourselves to what can be deontically described, then it would seem that persistence and revision are both rationally permissible. However, there is an important aspect of the rational response to a disagreement about reasons that has so far been left out of account. While, in the context of a disagreement about reasons, persistence and revision are both rationally permissible, sometimes at least, if acceptance is cognitive, there is something epistemically admirable about at least considering revising. After all, retaining belief on the grounds of conservativism, psychological necessity, and the like can seem like a reluctant capitulation to epistemic necessity. At any rate, acquiescing on such grounds is hardly a cognitive achievement. In contrast, a decision to reconsider manifests a responsiveness to reasons that is itself manifestly reasonable. Upon determining that his disagreement with Bernice is, at bottom, a disagreement about reasons, Edgar might be motivated to re-examine his reasons for accepting S. Edgar might inquire further into the grounds of his acceptance to determine whether, in light of his discussion with Bernice, his reasons for acceptance are good reasons. He might also inquire further to determine, in light of his discussion with Bernice, what, if anything, there is to Bernice's reasons for rejection. After all, Bernice might be onto something that so far eludes Edgar. While Edgar is not rationally required to inquire further into the grounds of acceptance, in the sense that his failure to do so would be epistemically blameworthy, there would be something epistemically admirable about his inquiring further. There is something cognitively virtuous about being motivated to inquire further into the grounds of acceptance in the face of a disagreement about reasons. If that is right, then there is a normative aspect of belief that is not describable in deontic vocabulary. Belief involves a cognitive virtue not describable in terms of rational permissibility. (See Rosen, 2001, for a similar suggestion.)

Two Kinds of Rational Norm

How are we to understand this? Here is one suggestion.

There are two kinds of rational norm.

The first kind of rational norm are those norms governing combinations of sentences that are candidates for acceptance. They take the form of principles determining whether combinations of sentences are rationally permissible, forbidden, or obligatory to accept. In a cognitive domain, they represent substantive judgments about the requirements of explanatory coherence on the epistemic state of a person at a time. A failure to conform to such a norm (by accepting a rationally forbidden combination of sentences, say) is irrational or, at the very least, epistemically blameworthy.

However, if acceptance is conceived as part of the broader activity of inquiry, where inquiry is one activity among many, then it is plausible that inquiry involves other kinds of norms as well. Just as there are rational norms governing combinations of sentences that are candidates for acceptance, it is plausible as well that there are rational norms governing the ends involved in inquiry. They represent the requirements on the ends to be adopted in changing one's epistemic state over time. So, for example, it is plausible to suppose that people who are motivated to inquire whether to accept S are rationally obliged to adopt means for determining whether to accept S consistent with other ends that they have adopted. Not only does inquiry, conceived as a complex activity, involve the adoption of appropriate instrumental ends, but it is plausible as well that there are noninstrumental ends internal to inquiry that people engaged in that activity are rationally obliged to adopt.

To see this, consider the following. Suppose that Edgar accepts certain sentences that are indirectly inconsistent. The sentences that he accepts are not directly inconsistent—he does not simultaneously accept both a sentence and its negation. Rather, he accepts certain sentences such that there is a possible argument, each step of which involves immediate implications of the sentences he accepts to a conclusion that leaves this pattern of acceptance directly inconsistent. Is Edgar thereby irrational? No. He might have good reasons for accepting each of these sentences and might not recognize that they are indirectly inconsistent. Suppose that Edgar comes to recognize that the sentences he accepts are indirectly inconsistent. Perhaps Bernice has explicitly given him the argument leading to direct inconsistency. Edgar would be rationally obliged as an inquirer to adopt the end of resolving this inconsistency. It is in this sense that resolving such inconsistency is an end internal to inquiry.

While Edgar may be obliged as an inquirer to adopt the end of resolving this inconsistency, it would not be irrational for Edgar to persist in his acceptance, saying to Bernice: 'That's really interesting, I'll have to think about that later, but right now I have to pick up the kids.' In the meantime, Edgar may persist in accepting the indirectly inconsistent sentences, taking care not to infer everything that is implied by them. (Recall, if you can, your initial reaction to the Liar paradox, or to Zeno's paradox.) Edgar's discovery that the sentences he accepts are indirectly inconsistent may rationally oblige him as an inquirer to adopt a certain end—namely, the end of resolving this inconsistency— but there is latitude in the fulfilment of this end. Resolving this inconsistency might be hampered by inevitable practical exigencies. After all, a person has a plurality of ends and the fulfilment of these must be rationally ordered. Rationally ordering adopted ends involves, among other things, prioritizing ends, scheduling means towards their fulfilment, and choosing means compatible with other ends. So the end of resolving the indirect inconsistency must in this way harmonize with other ends that Edgar has adopted (such as executing the daily routines involved in child-care). Whereas the content of the rational norm is purely epistemic—it requires only the adoption of an end internal to inquiry, the conditions for the fulfilment of this norm are not purely epistemic—acting on the obligatory end is constrained by considerations of practical coherence. Thus, there is latitude in the fulfilment of this end, and a failure to act towards its fulfilment merely lacks epistemic merit and is neither an instance of irrationality nor in any way epistemically blameworthy (though perhaps adopting the policy of never acting towards its fulfilment would be). I may not have resolved to my satisfaction the Liar paradox; I may never do so. But that does not make me irrational. My resolution of the paradox might be epistemically admirable, it might have epistemic merit; but my failure to do so is neither an instance of irrationality nor in any way epistemically blameworthy.

Inquiry thus involves two kinds of rational norm. On the one hand, there are rational norms governing combinations of sentences that are candidates for acceptance. They represent the requirements of explanatory coherence on the epistemic state of a person at a time. These are *strict* obligations. On the other hand, there are rational norms governing the ends involved in inquiry. They represent requirements on the ends to be adopted in changing one's epistemic state over time. These are *lax* obligations. Their laxity consists in the latitude involved in the fulfilment of these obligations, since an obligatory end is one end among many and a person's ends must be rationally ordered. The failure to fulfil a strict obligation is irrational or, at the very least, epistemically blameworthy. In contrast, any particular action taken to fulfil a lax obligation is epistemically meritorious, while any particular failure to act merely lacks epistemic merit and is neither an instance of irrationality nor epistemically blameworthy (though perhaps adopting the policy of never acting to fulfil the lax obligation would be). *Cognoscenti* will recognize this as an application to the epistemic case of the distinction between perfect and imperfect duties (see Kant, 1785/1999: 4: 421–3; 1797/1999: 6: 390–1.)

In a disagreement about reasons, persistence and revision are both rationally permissible. As such, the epistemic states involved in persistence and revision are in violation of no strict obligation. However, there is something admirable about at least considering revising, and this suggests the presence of a lax obligation, i.e. the presence of a rational obligation to adopt a certain end. What end could this be? Upon determining that his disagreement with Bernice is, at bottom, a disagreement about reasons, Edgar is under a lax obligation to inquire further into the grounds of acceptance. More precisely, given that he is interested in the truth of S, Edgar, in the context of a disagreement about reasons, has a reason to re-examine his reasons for accepting S, at least if his disputant is otherwise rational and reasonable, informed, and similarly interested in inquiring about S.

Let me explain. Even in the context of a disagreement about reasons, whether a person has a reason to inquire further depends on his interest in the truth of S. After all, 'The truth, the whole truth, and nothing but the truth' has never been a reasonable norm of inquiry. Absent some special interest, there is no reason to know whether Genghis Khan ever suffered from a hangnail, say. (See Harman, 1986: 55–6, for an explanation of the indispensability of interest in terms of the finite nature of inquirers.) However, given his interest in the truth of S, in the context of a disagreement about reasons, Edgar would have a motive to inquire further into the grounds of acceptance—or, at least, he would be so motivated if Bernice were otherwise rational and reasonable, informed, and similarly interested in inquiring about S. Obviously, Edgar would lack this motive if Bernice were irrational, or unreasonable, or ignorant, or were moved by ulterior motives unconnected with reasons for acceptance. But if she is none of these, Edgar would have a motive to inquire further into his grounds for acceptance to determine whether, in light of his discussion with Bernice, his reasons for acceptance are good reasons. Edgar would also have a motive to inquire further to determine, in light of his discussion with Bernice, what, if anything, there is to Bernice's reasons for rejection. After all, Bernice might be onto something that so far eludes Edgar. To inquire further is to strive to be responsive to what reasons there are. This would involve seriously considering the alternatives and so questioning the evidential status of initial appearances. While persistence is rationally permissible, Edgar must be prepared to bracket his full acceptance of S when re-examining his reasons for acceptance. Of course, there is latitude in the fulfilment of this end. Further inquiry is one end among many, and a person's ends must be rationally ordered—perhaps Edgar has more compelling immediate concerns. If, however, Edgar were to fulfil this end, he might satisfy himself with his acceptance of S, or he might suspend judgment concerning S, or might even reject S. Whatever the outcome, Edgar's noncomplacency in inquiring further would be epistemically admirable. Moreover, a failure to act towards the fulfilment of this end, to become responsive to what reasons there are, would merely lack epistemic merit and would be neither an instance of irrationality nor in any way epistemically blameworthy. Striving to be responsive to what reasons there are is, in this sense, a manifestation of cognitive virtue.

Two Kinds of Acceptance

The discussion so far provides preliminary support for the following claim:

Noncomplacency

If acceptance is cognitive, then, in the context of a disagreement about reasons, a person is under a lax obligation to inquire further into the grounds of acceptance. Specifically, if a person is interested in the truth of S, then, in the context of a disagreement about reasons, he would have a reason to re-examine his grounds for accepting S, at least if his disputant is otherwise rational and reasonable, informed, and similarly interested in inquiring about S.

Why should a disagreement about reasons motivate a person to inquire further into the grounds of acceptance? Perhaps the value of being reasonable constitutes a reason to inquire further. After all, in the face of a disagreement about reasons, to inquire further into the grounds of acceptance is to strive to be responsive to what reasons there are. Perhaps, then, in the context of a disagreement about reasons, if a person is interested in the truth of S, the value of being reasonable constitutes a reason to inquire further into the grounds of acceptance in the sense that part of what it is to be reasonable is to be so motivated in such circumstances (just as part of what it is to be benevolent is to be motivated by the good of others).

While initially plausible, noncomplacency is nevertheless controversial. A reasonable person interested in the truth of S would be motivated to inquire further if, in that context, it were open to reflective doubt about whether his reasons for acceptance were genuine reasons. But why must a disagreement about reasons invariably generate reflective doubt about the disputants' reasons? A disagreement about reasons would generate reflective doubt about the disputants' reasons if there were an acknowledged epistemic symmetry between them. But, in the context of any actual disagreement, it is plausibly always open to a person to simply deny that the symmetry obtains. Suppose that Bernice accepts that the Earth is flat and is ideally coherent in so accepting: Bernice is otherwise rational and reasonable, informed, and can offer what Edgar would regard as a question-begging argument for her acceptance of the flat Earth hypothesis. If Edgar is like us, he would reject any suggestion that there is a perfect epistemic symmetry between himself and Bernice but would maintain, instead, that he, and not Bernice, is appropriately related to the shape of the Earth. Thus, it is implausible to suppose that Edgar's disagreement about reasons with an ideally coherent flat-earther would generate reflective doubt about his reasons for rejecting the flat Earth hypothesis, and hence it is implausible to suppose that he would be motivated to inquire further into the grounds of his rejection, if interested. In the absence of such reflective doubt, a reasonable person interested in the truth of S may not be motivated to inquire further into the grounds of acceptance. In the absence of a special reason to doubt his reasons, a reasonable person interested in the truth of S may be satisfied that he is simply better placed to appreciate the facts.

The credibility of noncomplacency is thus subject to two apparently conflicting reactions: While initially plausible, it is controversial upon reflection. These apparently conflicting reactions would be reconciled, however, if it turned out that they were reactions to different things. Indeed, I believe that they are reactions to different things, for noncomplacency is ambiguous. They are two kinds of acceptance that are governed by distinct norms. Thus, noncomplacency can be understood as a claim about the norms governing one kind of acceptance or the other. Understood one way, this is plausible; understood the other way, it is controversial and plausibly false.

When a competent speaker accepts a sentence, he may accept that sentence for himself, but, importantly, he might do more than that. Not only may he accept the sentence for himself, but he might also accept that sentence on behalf of others. Acceptance for oneself is the object of individual inquiry. If a competent speaker accepts a sentence S for himself, then he takes himself to have sufficient reason to end his individual inquiry about S. So if Edgar accepts 'The UCL Philosophy Department is located at 19 Gordon Square' he has no further reason to inquire about the address. (Of course, he might still have a reason to ask Bernice what that address is—say, in order to determine whether Bernice knows that address. However, in asking Bernice, Edgar is not inquiring after the address; rather, he is inquiring after Bernice's knowledge of that address.) Acceptance for oneself is also the grounds of individual inquiry: if a competent speaker accepts S for himself, then he takes himself to have sufficient reason to rely on his acceptance of S in further theoretical and practical reasoning. So, for example, Edgar may rely on his acceptance of the address to estimate the time it would take to get there from his present location. Whereas acceptance for oneself is both the object and the grounds of individual inquiry, acceptance on behalf of others is the object and grounds of public inquiry: if a competent speaker accepts S on behalf of others, he takes himself to have sufficient reason to end public inquiry about S. Suppose Bernice asks Edgar for the address of the UCL Philosophy Department. If Edgar accepts the address on behalf of others, then, by his lights, there is no need for Bernice to inquire further—she may simply take his word for it. By his lights, his acceptance of the address can stand proxy for her own reasoning in inquiring about that address. Acceptance on behalf of others is also the grounds of public inquiry: if a competent speaker accepts S on behalf of others, he takes himself to have sufficient reason for others to rely on his acceptance of S in their own theoretical and practical reasoning. So, if Edgar accepts the address on behalf of others, then, by his lights, Bernice can rely on that address in her own theoretical and practical reasoning—she may, for example, rely on that address as a partial means of getting there.

The two kinds of acceptance involved in individual and public inquiry are governed by distinct norms. Thus, if a competent speaker accepts S on behalf of others, then he must coherently suppose, at least implicitly, that others do not accept reasons that would undermine his acceptance of S. (Harman, 1986: 51, observes that, in this respect, acceptance on behalf of others is like speaking on behalf of a group.) Suppose that Bernice asks Edgar where the UCL Philosophy Department is and he says that it is at 19 Gordon Square. Suppose, however, that Bernice has seen a flyer announcing that the Philosophy Department has moved from that address but she cannot now remember the 'new' address. Bernice would then accept a reason that undermines Edgar's acceptance of that address. Thus, Edgar would not be justified in accepting that address on behalf of others, because others, who are otherwise rational and reasonable, informed, and interested in inquiring about the address, accept undermining reasons and so reasonably reject that address. Nevertheless, Edgar could be justified in accepting the address for himself. Suppose that Edgar does not give full credence to the flyer. Perhaps he coherently supposes that it is a prank. Though Edgar cannot give Bernice a reason sufficient to rule out the evidence provided by the flyer, he does not give it credence, is coherent in not giving it credence, and continues to accept the 'old' address. While Edgar would not be justified in accepting the address on behalf of others, he would be justified in accepting that address for himself. This could be so only if acceptance for oneself and acceptance on behalf of others were governed by distinct norms.

This is further confirmed by the following. Suppose that Edgar is motivated to accept the address not only for himself but on behalf of others as well. (Suppose that Edgar and Bernice have a joint appointment there.) He might then look for evidence that would explain away the flyer. What explains his further inquiry is his motivation to accept the sentence on behalf of others coupled with the fact that he takes himself to be justified in accepting it for himself. After all, if Edgar did not take himself to be justified in accepting the sentence for himself, then why bother looking for evidence that would explain away the undermining reason provided by the flyer?

In a cognitive domain, being justified in accepting a sentence for oneself and being appropriately related to the facts is no guarantee that one has sufficient reason to accept the sentence on behalf of others. Suppose that Edgar were correct in supposing the flyer to be a prank. Edgar would be justified in accepting the 'old' address and is appropriately related to the facts. However, Edgar would not be justified in accepting this on behalf of others since others who are otherwise rational and reasonable, informed, and similarly motivated coherently accept undermining reasons and, hence, reasonably reject the 'old' address. So just because a person is appropriately related to the facts is no guarantee that he possesses sufficient reason to accept S on behalf of others.

Noncomplacency can be understood as a claim about the norms governing acceptance for oneself or as a claim about the norms governing acceptance on behalf of others. Understood as a claim about acceptance for oneself, noncomplacency is false. Absent reflective doubt about his reasons for accepting S, Edgar is under no obligation to inquire further into the grounds of acceptance even if he is interested in the truth of S, and the mere fact of a disagreement about reasons is in general insufficient to generate such reflective doubt, even if his disputant is otherwise rational and reasonable, informed, and interested in the acceptability of S. Suppose, however, that Edgar is interested in accepting S not only for himself, but on behalf of others as well. (Perhaps the truth or falsity of S is relevant to a joint endeavor that Edgar is undertaking with Bernice, or perhaps they are participants of a public inquiry engaged in competing research programs.) In accepting S on behalf of others, Edgar must coherently suppose, at least implicitly, that others who are otherwise rational and reasonable, informed, and interested in inquiring about S do not accept undermining reasons and hence, reasonably, reject S. Unfortunately, Bernice, who is otherwise rational and reasonable, informed, and interested in inquiring about S, accepts a reason that would undermine Edgar's acceptance of S. So, in the context of a disagreement about reasons, Edgar would lack sufficient reason to accept S on behalf of others even if he had sufficient reason to accept S for himself and were appropriately related to the facts. Since Edgar is interested in accepting S on behalf of others but lacks sufficient reason to do so, he would be motivated to inquire further into the grounds of acceptance to discover, if he can, grounds for accepting S that otherwise rational and reasonable, informed persons who are interested in inquiring about S could not reasonably reject. Inquiring further into the grounds of acceptance is an obligatory end of public inquiry for those engaged in a disagreement about reasons.

Moral Authority

Noncomplacency should be understood as a claim about the norms governing acceptance on behalf of others. The idea is that, if a person is interested in the truth of S, then, in the context of a disagreement about reasons, he would have a reason to re-examine his grounds for accepting S, at least if his disputant is otherwise rational and reasonable, informed, and similarly interested in inquiring about S. One distinctive feature of morality (or at least that part of morality that Gibbard, 1990, describes as 'morality in the narrow sense' and that Scanlon, 1998, describes as the domain of 'what we owe to each other') is its authority. Given the nature of its authority, moral acceptance is always acceptance on behalf of others. This is epistemically significant— for, taken together with noncomplacency, it has the following important consequence: if moral acceptance is cognitive, then, in the context of a disagreement about reasons, a person is under a lax obligation to inquire further into the grounds of moral acceptance.

Morality is authoritative. After all, while morality in some sense answers to our concerns, it is also in some sense independent of them. The authority of morality is manifest in the role it plays in moral discourse and in the cognitive psychology of competent speakers. A full account of that authority would involve specifying its source in a way that made it intelligible that it should exhibit that role. However, without giving a full account of moral authority, a partial description of the role it plays in moral discourse and in the cognitive psychology of competent speakers suffices to establish that moral acceptance is always acceptance on behalf of others.

In sincerely uttering a moral sentence that he understands, a competent speaker accepts the uttered moral sentence, and, in accepting it he accepts as well what reason is thereby provided. Bernice accepts that abortion is wrong and thereby accepts as well a reason not to have an abortion if pregnant. Moreover, the reason that Bernice accepts, if genuine, potentially overrides whatever reason she might have to have an abortion if pregnant. Not only do moral reasons potentially override whatever conflicting nonmoral reasons we have for acting in the given circumstance, but they can also potentially cancel such reasons in that circumstance (see Frankfurt, 1988, chapter 13; McDowell, 1998: 55–6, 91–3; and Scanlon, 1998: 156–7). Sometimes a moral reason doesn't so much outweigh nonmoral inclination as discounts it as a reason for acting in the given circumstance. It is implausible to claim that moral reasons necessarily override or cancel all conflicting nonmoral reasons. Suppose Bernice promises to meet Edgar, but an important and rare opportunity arises such that Bernice cannot avail herself of that opportunity if she fulfils her promise to Edgar. If the opportunity were important enough, and the promise was lightly given and of no great consequence to Edgar, then what reason there is to avail herself of that opportunity might outweigh the reason she has to meet Edgar (which is not, of course, to say that amends should not be made). While moral reasons do not always override or cancel conflicting nonmoral reasons, they very often do, and it is part of their nature and importance that they do. Thus, the moral reasons conveyed by our moral utterances often take precedence over conflicting nonmoral reasons:

> *Precedence*
> In uttering a moral sentence that he understands, a competent speaker conveys a reason to act in a given circumstance that potentially overrides or cancels any conflicting nonmoral reasons available in that circumstance. (Precedence is a variant of what Rawls, 1971, and Scanlon, 1998, describe as 'the priority of right.')

In accepting the wrongness of abortion, not only does Bernice accept a reason that takes precedence over nonmoral reasons, but she also takes the reason not to be contingent upon her acceptance of it. The acceptance of a moral reason is not a matter of taste. Of course, that something is to your taste is often a reason to prefer it. Bernice has a taste for westerns and distastes musicals. In deciding to watch one of two movies, a western and a musical, satisfying her taste for westerns constitutes a reason to watch the western rather than the musical. Moral reasons differ from matters of taste not in the sense that the former are reasons whereas the latter are not, but in the kind of reason they are.

According to Gibbard (1990: 164–6), if something is a matter of taste, satisfying that taste would not constitute a good reason if one lacked that taste. Bernice would not have a reason to watch the western if instead musicals were to her taste. In accepting something as a matter of taste, a person does not take that reason to apply independently of his accepting it: if he lacked that taste, he would lack that reason. (N.B.: The sense of 'taste' that Gibbard deploys is the one associated with the *de gustibus* motto and is distinct from the sense of taste whose standard Hume sought to establish.) Matters are different with moral reasons. In accepting that abortion is wrong, Bernice accepts a reason not to have an abortion if pregnant. Moreover, Bernice believes that she would still have a reason not to have an abortion if instead she accepted that abortion was morally permissible. The moral reason not to have an abortion applies, if it does at all, independently of Bernice's accepting it. Indeed, it applies, if it does at all, independently of *anyone's* accepting it. Emma does not accept that abortion is wrong because she is unsure about the moral status of abortion. Though Emma does not accept that abortion is wrong, Bernice believes that Emma has a reason not to have an abortion if pregnant even though Emma does not accept that reason. In accepting a moral reason, a person takes that reason to apply independently of a person's accepting it. The content of a moral reason is not linked to a person's acceptance of it the way a reason of taste is. If an action is wrong in a given circumstance, then everyone who is in that circumstance has a reason not to perform that action, whether or not they accept that reason:

> *Noncontingency*
> In uttering a moral sentence that he understands, the existence of the reason conveyed is not contingent upon the speaker's or anyone else's accepting it.

In accepting the wrongness of abortion, not only does Bernice accept a reason that takes precedence over nonmoral reasons, that is not contingent upon her acceptance of it, but she also believes that she has good reason to accept that it is wrong and that this is a reason, not only for her, but for everyone else as well. Emma, unlike Bernice, does not accept that abortion is wrong, but from Bernice's perspective Emma is thereby unreasonable, if not indeed irrational. Bernice regards Emma as unreasonable in the sense that Emma is not responding to what reason there is to accept the wrongness of abortion. (She is not, however, irrational, at least not in the narrow sense of acting at variance with a reason she accepts.) The putative reason that Bernice has for accepting that abortion is wrong is a reason for everyone to accept that abortion is wrong, or would be if it were a genuine reason. We might describe this as *well-groundedness:* In uttering a moral sentence that he understands, the reason a competent speaker has, if sincere, for accepting the uttered moral sentence applies not only to the speaker but to everyone else as well.

There is a complication, however. Emma is unsure about the moral status of abortion. Suppose, however, she comes to regard Bernice's moral opinion as authoritative in this instance. Perhaps Emma trusts Bernice's moral sensibility more than her own in the given circumstance. While Emma is sure that Bernice has a good reason to accept the wrongness of abortion, Emma herself remains unclear about that reason—she is unclear about which features of her circumstance count as a reason for the impermissibility of abortion, or even why these features should have this normative significance. Emma's reason for accepting the wrongness of abortion is that Bernice advises her that it is wrong. However, this is not a reason for someone who does not trust Bernice's moral sensibility the way Emma does. So Emma's reason for accepting the wrongness of abortion is not a reason for others to accept the wrongness of abortion. Thus, well-groundedness is false as presently formulated. Can this principle be reformulated to accommodate this complexity? Emma's reason for accepting the wrongness of abortion is that Bernice advises her that it is wrong. Bernice's advice is a reason, if it is, because Bernice has good reason for the wrongness of abortion. This reason, if genuine, is a *grounding* reason, since it is the grounds for the wrongness of abortion, and is a reason not only for Bernice but for everyone else as well to accept the wrongness of abortion. Bernice's advice is reason to accept the wrongness of abortion because Emma believes that Bernice has reasons that ground the wrongness of abortion. Although Emma is unclear about the nature of these grounds, she is nevertheless sure of their existence. Moral testimony can provide access to grounding reasons even to persons who lack an adequate conception of those reasons. Moreover, it is these grounding reasons, if they exist, that are reasons for everyone to accept the wrongness of abortion and, hence, are reasons to accept the wrongness of abortion on behalf of others. The principle should be reformulated as follows:

> *Well-groundedness*
> In uttering a moral sentence that he understands, the grounding reason a competent speaker directly or indirectly has, if sincere, for accepting the uttered moral sentence applies not only to the speaker but to everyone else as well. So, in sincerely uttering a moral sentence that he understands, a competent speaker accepts that sentence on behalf of others.

There is one further feature of moral authority that is worth emphasizing. In accepting the wrongness of abortion, not only does Bernice accept a reason that takes precedence over non-moral reasons, that is not contingent upon her acceptance of it, for which there are grounds not only for her but for everyone to accept, but in uttering 'Abortion is wrong' Bernice is *demanding* that everyone accept that it is wrong. Stevenson (1937, 1944) highlights this feature of moral authority by the 'do so as well' component of his analysis. According to Stevenson, Bernice, in claiming that abortion is wrong, not only represents herself as disapproving of abortion, but also demands that others do so as well. In making a moral utterance, a competent speaker demands that his audience accept the uttered moral sentence and so come to respond affectively in the relevant manner. The relevant response need not be the same as the speaker's: it may make sense for the hearer to feel guilty and the speaker to feel angry, say, but if it does this difference is grounded in their different relative positions in the circumstance and the normative appearance it presents:

> *Demand*
> In uttering a moral sentence that he understands, a competent speaker demands that his audience accept the uttered moral sentence.

While Stevenson emphasizes the demand conveyed by moral utterance, what is perhaps missing in his account is the recognition that the reasons that ground the acceptance of the uttered moral sentence are linked with this demand. Thus, MacIntyre writes:

Stevenson . . . understood very clearly that saying 'I disapprove of this; do so as well!' does not have the same force as 'This is bad!' He noted that a kind of prestige attaches to the latter, which does not attach to the former. What he did not note however—precisely because he viewed emotivism as a theory of meaning—is that the prestige derives from the fact that the use of 'That is bad!' implies an appeal to an objective and impersonal standard in a way in which 'I disapprove of this; do so as well!' does not. (MacIntyre, 1981: 19–20)

Stevenson's account of moral utterance fails to capture its authority, since he does not link the conversational demand it conveys with the reasons for accepting the uttered moral sentence. This is plausibly the source of the traditional criticism that moral utterance, as Stevenson conceives of it, is a form of manipulation—since competent speakers demand that others adopt the relevant emotional attitude without providing them with a reason for adopting that attitude. The conversational demand that others accept the uttered moral sentence is justified only if the speaker possesses a grounding reason for accepting the uttered moral sentence that applies not only to himself but to everyone else as well. The conversational demand is justified only if the speaker has sufficient reason to accept the uttered moral sentence on behalf of others. Demanding that others accept the uttered moral sentence may require that the speaker possess a grounding reason that applies not only to himself but to everyone else as well, but the possession of a grounding reason only potentially justifies demanding that others accept the moral sentence. So, for example, a competent speaker would not be justified in demanding that another accept a moral sentence, even if he possessed a grounding reason, if, in that context, so demanding would humiliate the other.

Given the nature of moral authority, moral acceptance is always acceptance on behalf of others and so is subject to the appropriate norms. David Hume puts the point this way:

When a man denominates another his *enemy*, his *rival*, his *antagonist*, his *adversary*, he is understood to speak the language of self-love, and to express sentiments, peculiar to himself, and arising from his particular circumstances and situation. But when he bestows on any man the epithets of *vicious* or *odious* or *depraved*, he then speaks another language, and expresses sentiments, in which, he expects, all his audience are to concur with him. He must here, therefore, depart from his private and particular situation, and must chuse a point of view, common to him and others. (Hume 1751/1988: section 9)

Reacting to Moral Disagreement

Given the nature of moral authority, moral acceptance is always acceptance on behalf of others. Not only does well-groundedness entail that accepting a moral sentence involves accepting that sentence on behalf of others, but the conversational demand conveyed by moral utterance is intelligible only if sincerely uttering a moral sentence involves accepting that sentence on behalf of others. This is epistemically significant; for, taken together with noncomplacency, it has the following important consequence: if moral acceptance is cognitive, then, in the context of a disagreement about reasons, a person is under a lax obligation to inquire further into the grounds of acceptance. By contraposition, it follows that if, in the context of a disagreement about reasons, a person is not under a lax obligation to inquire further into the grounds of moral acceptance, then moral acceptance is noncognitive. In this section I will argue for noncognitivism on just these grounds.

Edgar and Bernice disagree about the moral status of abortion. Whereas Bernice accepts the wrongness of abortion, Edgar is a complacent liberal moralist and accepts that abortion is permissible. Upon discussing the matter, Edgar and Bernice discover that their disagreement is a disagreement about reasons. Edgar reasons as follows:

Everyone has a right over their own person and their own body. Given the nature of these rights, when an embryo is essentially part of the mother's body, the mother has the right to make her own uncoerced decision on whether she will have an abortion or not. Therefore, abortion is morally permissible.... (MacIntyre, 1981: 6–7)

So Edgar, implicitly at least, accepts a principle that counts a certain feature of the circumstance, the embryo being essentially part of the mother's body, as a reason to accept the permissibility of abortion. Bernice, however, rejects this principle. Bernice reasons instead as follows:

I cannot will that my mother should have had an abortion when she was pregnant with me, except perhaps if it had been certain that the embryo was dead or gravely damaged. But if I cannot will this in my own case, how can I consistently deny to others the right to life I claim for myself? I would break the so-called Golden Rule unless I denied that a mother has in general a right to an abortion. (MacIntyre, 1981: 6–7)

From Bernice's perspective, the embryo being essentially part of the mother's body has a different normative significance. As a consequence, Edgar and Bernice disagree about what would count as a reason for accepting or rejecting the sentence 'Abortion is permissible.' Edgar and Bernice's disagreement about the moral status of abortion is, at bottom, a disagreement about reasons.

In uttering 'Abortion is permissible' Edgar demands, implicitly at least, that his audience accept that sentence. So Edgar must accept that sentence on behalf of others if his utterance is sincere. Indeed, Edgar is sincere. He accepts 'Abortion is permissible' on behalf of others for he takes himself to have access to a grounding reason that is a reason to accept that sentence not only for himself, but for everyone else as well. Bernice, like Edgar, is motivated to accept on behalf of others a claim about the moral status of abortion. Supposing that she is an intelligent and articulate spokesperson, Bernice might strike Edgar as an otherwise rational and reasonable, informed human being who coherently accepts a reason that, if genuine, would undermine his acceptance of the permissibility of abortion. Nevertheless, Edgar feels no embarrassment about this. His persistence in his liberal morality is unflinching. Edgar is intransigent in the sense that he lacks a motivation to inquire further into the grounds of moral acceptance. Nor is Edgar alone in this. I suspect that we too would be unmoved by such a disagreement. Our own persistence in liberal morality would be unflinching as well. We too would be intransigent in the sense of lacking a motivation to inquire further into the grounds of moral acceptance. In normal circumstances, we are under no obligation to re-examine the foundations of moral claims that we accept as unproblematic even if they are disputed by otherwise rational and reasonable, informed, and interested people who coherently accept reasons that, if genuine, would undermine them.

I am not making an empirical claim about the actual extent of moral intransigence—that would require a sensitive interpretation of a moral sociology that has yet to be written; rather, I am making a conceptual claim about the norms that actually govern moral acceptance: Given the norms that we actually accept, it is intelligible to fail to be motivated to inquire further. If we can conceive of cases where such intransigence is intelligible, then it must be so at least by the norms governing moral acceptance that we actually accept and tacitly appeal to in so conceiving. Not only is it intelligible that one, as a matter of fact, takes no positive steps towards re-examining the grounds of moral acceptance— after all, one might have more compelling immediate concerns; but it is intelligible as well that one should lack this motivation altogether. And if the failure to adopt the end of further inquiry is intelligible, then we are under no rational obligation to adopt this end, at least by the norms of moral acceptance that we actually, if implicitly, accept.

As an illustration of this, consider Hilary Putnam's admirable description of the deep political disagreement between Nozick and himself:

But what of the fundamentals on which one cannot *agree*? It would be dishonest to pretend that one thinks that there are no better and worse views *here*. I don't think that it is just a matter of *taste* whether one thinks that the obligation of the community to treat its members with compassion takes precedence over property rights; nor does my co-disputant. Each of us regards the other as lacking, at this level, a certain kind of sensitivity and perception. To be perfectly honest, there is in each of us something akin to *contempt*, not for the other's *mind*—for we each have the highest regard for each other's minds—nor for the other as a *person*—, for I have more respect for my colleague's honesty, integrity, kindness, etc., than I do for that of many people who agree with my 'liberal' political views—but for a certain complex of emotions and judgments in the other. (Putnam, 1981: 165)

Putnam should be commended for his candour here. What Putnam holds in something akin to contempt is Nozick's moral sensibility ('a certain complex of emotions and judgments in the other')—a moral sensibility that privileges property rights over what Putnam regards as the compassionate treatment of the less well off. Nozick is a reasonable and interested person who accepts reasons that, if genuine, would undermine Putnam's commitment to liberal morality. But if Putnam holds Nozick's moral sensibility in something akin to contempt, what motivation would *Nozick's* accepting an undermining reason provide *Putnam* for inquiring further into the grounds of moral acceptance? None. Thus, the reaction that Putnam carefully describes is a manifestation of moral intransigence. The important point, however, is that Putnam's reaction is not obviously unintelligible. And if it isn't, then under such circumstances we would be under no obligation to re-examine the foundations of the liberal morality we accept, if we do.

Relativity and Error

The argument from intransigence can be summarized as follows. If acceptance were cognitive, then, in the context of a disagreement about reasons, a person would be under a lax obligation to inquire further into the grounds of acceptance. This, however, is plausible only if acceptance is understood as acceptance on behalf of others. Given the nature of its authority, however, moral acceptance is always acceptance on behalf of others. So if moral acceptance were cognitive, then in the context of a disagreement about reasons, a person would be under a lax obligation to inquire further into the grounds of moral acceptance. However, in the context of a disagreement about reasons, a person is under no obligation to inquire further into the grounds of moral acceptance. Therefore, moral acceptance must be noncognitive.

A moral relativist might object that the argument from intransigence is unsound. According to moral relativism, moral acceptance is belief in a moral proposition; it is just that the moral proposition has relative truth-conditions. Thus, if Edgar accepts that abortion is permissible, he believes that abortion is permissible, but that proposition is true only relative to a moral framework: abortion is represented as permissible only relative to the moral framework in which Edgar participates. Similarly, if Bernice accepts that abortion is wrong, she believes that abortion is wrong, but that proposition is true only relative to a moral framework: abortion is represented as wrong only relative to the moral framework in which Bernice participates. Suppose that Edgar and Bernice participate in distinct moral frameworks. A disagreement about reasons would not motivate Edgar to inquire further into the grounds of moral acceptance, any more than a disagreement about the perceived location of a rainbow would motivate him to inquire about the 'true,' or perspective-independent, location of the rainbow. Thus, according to the envisioned moral relativist, moral acceptance is cognitive, but in a disagreement about reasons a person is under no obligation to inquire further into the grounds of acceptance. The relativist provides an alternative explanation for the intelligibility of intransigence, and one that is consistent with cognitivism. He would thus object that the argument from intransigence is unsound because it involves a false premise:

> If moral acceptance is cognitive, then, in the context of a disagreement about reasons, a person is under a lax obligation to inquire further into the grounds of moral acceptance.

The relativist makes a natural assumption—that, in a disagreement about reasons, the disputants participate in distinct moral frameworks. However, it is unclear why this assumption is invariably true. Why couldn't a disagreement about reasons arise within a single moral framework? After all, such moral frameworks, if they exist, are the contingent products of human culture and history. It is thus implausible to suppose that they are complete in the sense of partitioning the practical alternatives open to a person as permissible, forbidden, or obligatory in every possible circumstance. Unforeseen circumstances may give rise to practical alternatives unclassified by the moral framework. Indeed, there may be different ways of naturally extending the given framework to take these into account. But if this is the basis of the disagreement about reasons, then there is a clear sense in which the disputants participate in the same moral framework: they would be disagreeing about how to extend the incomplete moral framework that they share.

This is not the only way a disagreement about reasons can arise within a single moral framework. Consider a disagreement about the justice of an institutional policy. The disputants might disagree, for example, about the justice of an institutional policy, even though they agree about the description of the circumstance and the probable outcomes, and share substantially the same conception of justice. They might nevertheless reasonably disagree about how to apply the principles of justice they share to the circumstance as they commonly understand it. They would be engaged in a disagreement in reasons despite their common moral framework. If a disagreement about reasons can arise within a single moral framework, then, at least in these cases, the relativist loses his explanation for why the disputants are under no obligation to inquire further into the grounds of acceptance.

The relativist objection rests on a false, though natural, assumption—that in a disagreement about reasons the disputants participate in distinct moral frameworks. However, even if this difficulty were avoided, the relativist would face serious difficulties. The relativist denies the following:

If moral acceptance is cognitive, then, in the context of a disagreement about reasons, a person is under a lax obligation to inquire further into the grounds of moral acceptance.

However, this was a consequence of two claims:

Noncomplacency
If acceptance is cognitive and on behalf of others, then, in the context of a disagreement about reasons, a person is under a lax obligation to inquire further into the grounds of acceptance.

Authority
Given its authority, moral acceptance is always acceptance on behalf of others.

This is the basis of a dilemma: the relativist must deny either noncomplacency or authority. Recall that noncomplacency was urged on general grounds. So, if a relativist were to deny it, his relativism would no longer be confined to moral inquiry, but would instead be a form of epistemic relativism more generally. Epistemic relativism, however, is a controversial doctrine and should not be accepted merely by reflecting on the intelligibility of moral intransigence (but see Rosen, 2001, for a recent defense). If, on the other hand, the relativist were to deny authority—that moral acceptance is always acceptance on behalf of others—either by denying it outright or by restricting its scope, say, to those who are co-participants in a moral framework, he risks giving an unacceptably deflationary account of moral authority. These are serious difficulties, if not, perhaps, decisive ones. However, they suffice to cast doubt on the claim that relativist's alternative is clearly the better explanation of the intelligibility of moral intransigence. Indeed, the prevalence of relativist rhetoric in a moral culture might be a symptom of its noncognitive nature, since it might be a confused acknowledgment of the intelligibility of moral intransigence that is best explained by noncognitivism.

An error theorist might also object to the soundness of the argument, though on different grounds.

Noncognitivists are committed to a nonmoral explanation of moral acceptance. But noncognitivists are not the only ones with this explanatory commitment. Consider the kind of error theory that Mackie (1977) espoused. Mackie held that moral facts are 'queer' (or would be if there were any) and best not believed in. So, according to Mackie, there are no moral facts. But if there are no moral facts, then a competent speaker's acceptance of a moral sentence cannot be subject to a moral explanation. Moral acceptance might be belief, but the explanation for moral acceptance cannot be that the moral facts are thus and so and that the speaker is justified in believing them to be, as the realist maintains. The explanation for why a speaker accepts a moral sentence must be a nonmoral explanation. Indeed, the nonmoral explanation might take the form that noncognitivists recommend. Sometimes belief can be explained in terms of the noncognitive attitudes of the believer. Wishful thinking is a case in point. Bernice believed that England would win the World Cup. However, her belief was not the product of an impartial assessment of comparative merit; rather, she believed that England would win because she desperately wanted them to. Similarly, the error theorist might claim that, in accepting a moral sentence, a speaker believes the proposition expressed not because the moral facts are as the proposition represents them to be, but because of the noncognitive attitudes of the speaker. So for example the error theorist might claim that Edgar believes that it is good to help those in need, not because helping those in need instantiates the property of goodness, but rather because of his compassion for the needy.

Suppose an error theorist maintains that moral acceptance is subject not only to a nonmoral explanation but to a noncognitive explanation as well. This might seem to undermine the case for noncognitivism. Suppose moral sentences were best explained in terms of the noncognitive attitudes of the speaker. This is consistent with the possibility that a competent speaker, in accepting what he does on the basis of his noncognitive attitudes, is getting things systematically wrong.

The alleged difficulty is a product of not clearly distinguishing noncognitivism from noncognitive explanations of moral acceptance. It is one thing to claim that moral acceptance is subject to a noncognitive explanation; it is quite another to claim that moral acceptance is noncognitive. To claim that moral acceptance is noncognitive is to make a claim about the norms governing acceptance. If moral acceptance is in this sense noncognitive, then of course a competent speaker's acceptance of a moral claim will be subject to a noncognitive explanation. However, as our discussion of the error theory reveals, just because moral acceptance is subject to a noncognitive explanation, it does not follow that moral acceptance is noncognitive. Perhaps acceptance is belief. The fact that moral acceptance is best explained by the noncognitive attitudes of the speaker would then show only that the norms governing acceptance were being systematically violated. A noncognitive explanation of moral acceptance does not by itself establish the truth of noncognitivism. However, the conclusion of the argument from intransigence is not merely that moral acceptance is best explained by some attitude other than moral belief. Rather, as the intelligibility of moral intransigence reveals, the norms governing moral acceptance differ from the norms appropriate to belief. Thus, the error theorist's objection mistakes a conceptual claim about the norms that actually govern moral acceptance for an empirical claim about what actually explains moral acceptance. It ignores the way in which a potential explanatory difference between cognitivists and noncognitivists is a manifestation of a more fundamental normative difference.

The Argument from Aspect Shift

The argument from intransigence, if sound, only establishes the noncognitivist's distinctive denial. It remains silent, however, about the nature of the attitudes involved in moral acceptance. It is natural to ask: if moral acceptance is noncognitive, what kind of attitude is it? In this section we will consider a supplementary argument for noncognitivism, the argument from aspect shift, which has an informative conclusion about the nature of these attitudes. While not, even suitably elaborated, a full and substantive account of the nature of moral acceptance, the conclusion nevertheless provides positive information about the kind of attitudes involved in accepting a moral sentence.

So far, in discussing disagreements about reasons, we have naturally focused on interpersonal disagreement. However, corresponding to public moral conflict there is the possibility of private conflict: there could be intrapersonal disagreement corresponding to interpersonal disagreement. Specifically, in arguing for noncognitivism, the suggestion is that a disagreement about reasons might be approached from the deliberative perspective of a single practical reasoner.

There is an aspect of the phenomenology of intrapersonal conflict that is presently relevant. Emma is unsure about the moral status of abortion. She is genuinely undecided about the permissibility of abortion, even having considered Edgar and Bernice's explicit arguments. When Emma reflects on the rights people have over their own persons, certain features of her circumstance become salient and present a certain normative appearance. Specifically, in rehearsing Edgar's argument, Emma has a tendency to focus on a material feature of the circumstance, the embryo being essentially a part of the mother, and a tendency to count this a reason for permitting abortion as well as a tendency to rule out other features of the circumstance, such as the inability to universalize the decision to abort, as a reason for forbidding abortion. However, when she reflects on the value of her decisions, universalizing different features of her circumstance become salient and seem to have a different normative appearance. Specifically, in rehearsing Bernice's argument, Emma has a tendency to focus on a formal feature of the circumstance, the inability to universalize a decision to abort, and a tendency to count that as a reason for forbidding abortion as well as a tendency to rule out other features of the circumstance, such as the embryo being essentially part of the mother, as a reason for permitting abortion. The rival arguments differently structure the reasons apparently available in the given circumstance. From the perspective of rights, certain features of the circumstance count as reasons and others are ruled out. From the perspective of universalizability, different features of the circumstance count as reasons and yet others are ruled out (compare Nagel, 1979: essay 9.) Since she cannot reconcile these arguments in a single coherent normative framework, Emma, in moving between these distinct normative perspectives, experiences what can only be described as a normative aspect shift: in moving between these distinct normative perspectives, different features of her circumstance become salient and present a different normative appearance. Thus Ulrich, the protagonist of Musil's *The Man without Qualities* explains:

I maintained that a general who for strategic reasons sends his battalions to certain doom is a murderer, if you think of them as thousands of mothers' sons, but that he immediately becomes something else seen from another perspective, such as, for example, the necessity of sacrifice, or the insignificance of life's short span. (Musil, 1995: 295)

Noncognitivism provides the best explanation for the normative aspect shift involved in the phenomenology of intrapersonal conflict. Consider the way a normative perspective structures a person's moral consciousness. Adopting a normative perspective involves a tendency for certain features of the circumstance to become salient in perception, thought, and imagination, and a tendency for these features to present a certain complex normative appearance. A normative perspective structures a person's moral consciousness in just the way that a certain kind of affect structures a person's consciousness.

Consider erotic desire. Edgar walks into a crowded room and is immediately struck by the presence of his beloved, Bernice. Bernice is immediately perceptually salient. Edgar experiences Bernice as quite literally standing out of the crowd. Bernice's salience is not merely confined to his perception. Edgar has, as well, a tendency to focus on Bernice in thought and imagination. Not only is Bernice salient, but her desirability is also manifest in a phenomenologically vivid manner. Indeed in his vulnerable moments this phenomenologically vivid sense of Bernice's desirability can be unbearable and thus has a tendency to be shy-making. Not only does Edgar have a tendency to see Bernice as desirable, but he also has a tendency to rule out from consideration certain features of Bernice that, to others at least, might count against her desirability. So, for example, he has a tendency to overlook certain annoying habits such as Bernice's penchant for chewing on pens when concentrating. It is not that Bernice's pen chewing is outweighed by her manifest desirability. At least in this instance, for Edgar it is not even an issue. Indeed, Edgar is so far gone that he sees Bernice's pen chewing as contributing to her unique charm. So Edgar's desiring Bernice involves, among other things, a tendency for Bernice to become salient in perception, thought, and imagination as well as a tendency for her to present a certain normative appearance. Indeed, Scanlon (1998: chapter 1) characterizes a certain kind of affect, what he calls *desire in the directed attention sense*, precisely in terms of these effects. Specifically, according to Scanlon, a desire in the directed attention sense involves a tendency to focus on the object of desire as well as a tendency for the object of desire to appear in a favourable light. (There is a sense in which the label 'desire in the directed attention' sense is inapt—it suggests a too narrow construal of the relevant kind of affect. Specifically, it suggests that the constituent normative appearance is invariably positive. However, whatever Scanlon's intention, I am not assuming that the object of the affect invariably appears in a *favorable* light, only that there is a tendency for the object of the affect to have a certain normative appearance, whether or not that appearance is positive.) So it seems that a normative perspective structures a person's moral consciousness in just the way a certain kind of affect, desire in the directed attention sense, structures a person's consciousness.

This might be so if a person's normative perspective were just their being disposed to respond affectively in the relevant manner. If that is right, then the normative aspect shift involved in the phenomenology of intrapersonal conflict is subject to a noncognitive explanation. From the perspective of rights, certain features of the circumstance count as reasons and others are excluded. From the perspective of universalizability, different features of the circumstance count as reasons and yet others are excluded. Emma, in moving between these distinct normative perspectives, experiences a normative aspect shift. This normative aspect shift is nothing other than Emma's vacillating between distinct and incompatible affective responses to her circumstance. In being unclear about the moral status of abortion, Emma quite literally does not know what to feel about it. (Thus Hume, 1740/2003: 3.1.2: 'Morality, therefore, is more properly felt than judg'd of.')

This hypothesis receives some independent support by the rhetorical strategies deployed when reasons give out in basic moral disagreement. Thus, Edgar, in trying to persuade Bernice of the permissibility of abortion after she has listened to and rejected his explicit argument, might do any and all of the following: he might exhort Bernice to see it like this..., to consider certain pertinent analogies as well as certain cases whose description has a narrative structure that expresses Edgar's feelings about abortion—he might even resort to browbeating. These and other rhetorical strategies are essentially literary devices for focusing the audience's attention on certain features of the circumstance and presenting those features in a certain normative light. Such rhetorical strategies, when artfully deployed, get the audience to respond affectively in the relevant way to the given circumstance—they frame the perspective of the audience so as to induce the relevant affect. By such means Edgar might try to instill in Bernice what Putnam (1981: 165) describes as a 'certain complex of emotions and judgments.' In this way, a familiar, intuitionist rhetoric can have a noncognitive use. (See MacIntyre, 1981: chapter 2; but see McDowell, 1998, essays 3, 10, for a different interpretation of this rhetoric.)

So far, the relevant kind of affect has been characterized in terms of its functional role, i.e. in terms of the tendency for certain features of the circumstance to become salient in perception, thought, and imagination and the tendency for these features to present a certain normative appearance. But why do these effects hang together? What is it about the nature of this attitude that explains and renders intelligible that it should have this functional role?—Johnston (2001) forcefully presses this question. McDowell (1998: essays 3, 10) suggests that it is 'natural' for the noncognitivist to conceive of this attitude as a mixed state, a noncognitive refinement of sensing, where the noncognitive component is the source of the normative appearance. McDowell has done much to discredit the claim that the relevant kind of affect can be understood as a mixed state involving perceptual and noncognitive components that can be independently specified. Even if this kind of account were untenable and were the only substantive specification of the relevant kind of affect available to the noncognitivist, why should the noncognitivist provide a substantive account of desire in the directed attention sense? Why should desire in the directed attention sense be understood as an attitude whose nature can be specified independently of its functional role, and can explain and render intelligible why this attitude has that functional role?

If the affect were conceived to be a particular event in a person's consciousness (a 'feeling,' in the philosopher's sense), then it would be reasonable to assume that its nature would be manifest in the way it structures a person's consciousness, and so reasonable to assume that the nature of the affect would explain and render intelligible the tendency of the object of the affect to become salient and the tendency for it to present a certain normative appearance. However, to assume at the outset that the affect is a particular conscious event is to overlook a metaphysical option available to the noncognitivist. Perhaps the affect is not some particular event in a person's consciousness, but the way in which events in the person's consciousness are structured. The suggestion is that there is nothing more to being an affect of the relevant kind than the tendency for certain features of the circumstance to become salient in perception, thought, and imagination, and the tendency for these features to present a certain normative appearance. The *minimalist* denies that a person's being in an affective state consists in some further fact over and above the relevant way in which the person's consciousness is structured. Minimalism is thus the analogue in the philosophy of mind of T. S. Eliot's notion of the 'objective correlative':

The only way of expressing emotion in the form of art is by finding an 'objective correlative'; in other words, a set of objects, a situation, a chain of events which shall be the formula of that *particular* emotion; such that when the external facts, which must terminate in sensory experience, are given, the emotion is immediately evoked. (Eliot, 1932: 145)

This conception of emotional expression in art is the basis of Eliot's criticism of *Hamlet*: the emotion that has Hamlet in its grips is inexpressible precisely because it is a further fact over and above the structure of events in the narrative, and for this reason Eliot reckons the play a failure:

If you examine any of Shakespeare's more successful tragedies, you will find this exact equivalence; you will find that the state of mind of Lady Macbeth walking in her sleep has been communicated to you by a skilful accumulation of imagined sensory impressions; the words of Macbeth on hearing of his wife's death strike us as if, given the sequence of events, these words were automatically released by the last event in the series. The artistic 'inevitability' lies in this complete adequacy of the external to the emotion; and this is precisely what is deficient in *Hamlet*. Hamlet (the man) is dominated by an emotion which is inexpressible, because it is in *excess* of the facts as they appear. (Eliot, 1932: 145)

Just as Eliot contends that it is the structure of the events in the narrative ('the facts as they appear'), and not some further fact, that constitutes the expression of emotion, the minimalist contends that it is the structure of the events in a person's consciousness, and not some further fact, that constitutes the relevant affect.

McDowell (1998: essays 3, 10) suggests that it is 'natural' for the noncognitivist to conceive of this attitude as a mixed state, a noncognitive refinement of sensing, where the cognitive and noncognitive components can be independently specified and where the nature of this mixed state explains and renders intelligible the way a person's consciousness is structured. According to the minimalist, desire in the directed attention sense is a mixed state: it is a noncognitive attitude that involves thoughts and perceptions about the morally salient features of the circumstance. However, these attitudes are not distinct and so cannot be independently specified; nor can they explain the way they structure a person's consciousness. The thoughts and perceptions involved in moral acceptance are events in a person's consciousness whose structure constitutes the relevant affect. So, even if a substantive account of desire in the directed attention sense were unavailable to the noncognitivist for the reasons McDowell describes, a noncognitivist might still claim that the relevant affect is nothing other than the tendency for certain features of the circumstance to become salient in perception, thought, and imagination and the tendency for them to present a certain complex normative appearance.

If one accepts the minimalist account of desire in the directed attention sense, then the case for noncognitivism is strengthened. It would no longer be a question of noncognitivism providing the best explanation for the normative aspect shift: minimalism and the claim that the affect is noncognitive would entail a noncognitive account of normative aspect shift.

Accepting a moral sentence will seem reasonable, given an appropriate background normative perspective. From the normative perspective of rights, accepting that abortion is permissible might seem reasonable. From the perspective of universalizability, accepting that abortion is wrong might seem reasonable. Given that the adoption of a normative perspective is just a matter of appropriately configuring one's affective sensibility, it is plausible that moral acceptance is itself noncognitive. Moreover, if it is, then it is no surprise that it should lack a cognitive virtue that genuine belief displays.

Conclusion

Moral acceptance is noncognitive. Specifically, moral acceptance centrally involves a certain kind of affect, what Scanlon (1998) describes as a desire in the directed attention sense. In accepting a moral sentence that he understands, a competent speaker reconfigures his affective sensibility so as to render salient, in a phenomenologically vivid manner, the moral reasons apparently available in the circumstance, as he understands it. In accepting a moral sentence that he understands, a competent speaker quite literally decides how he feels about things. It is the structure of a person's moral consciousness, and not some further fact, that constitutes the relevant kind of affect. The relevant affect is nothing over and above the tendency for certain features of the circumstance to become salient in perception, thought, and imagination, and for these to present a certain complex normative appearance. Specifically, certain features of the circumstance become salient and appear to be reasons for acting, while other features potentially cease to be salient and can appear to be outweighed or even ruled out as reasons for doing otherwise, even if, in normal circumstances, they would count as such reasons. The salient features appear to be reasons that are not contingent upon our acceptance of them. Moreover, potentially distinct features of the circumstance become salient and appear to be reasons for accepting the moral sentence, and these reasons directly or indirectly involve grounding reasons, reasons that ground the deontic status of the relevant practical alternatives. These grounding reasons appear to be reasons not only for the speaker, but for everyone else as well. They appear to be sufficient reason for accepting that sentence on behalf of others. From this perspective, the competent speaker can seem justified in demanding that others accept the moral sentence and so come to respond affectively in the relevant manner. The affects centrally involved in moral acceptance are in this way essentially other regarding.

2

The Pragmatic Fallacy

Introduction

Noncognitivism is a claim about the attitudes involved in moral acceptance:

Noncognitivism
Accepting a moral sentence wholly consists in attitudes other than belief in a moral proposition.

Thus, on the present account, moral acceptance is not belief in a moral proposition but a certain kind of affect, a desire in the directed attention sense. Whereas noncognitivism, in its primary sense, is a claim about moral acceptance, as standardly developed, it is part of a syndrome of ideas that include positive and negative claims about moral semantics. The negative claim is that the content of a moral sentence does not consist in a moral proposition—a proposition that attributes moral properties to things:

Nonfactualism
The content of a moral sentence does not consist in any moral proposition expressed, for it expresses none.

Standard noncognitivists do not simply endorse this denial; in addition, they make a positive claim about the semantics of moral discourse. Typically, they claim that the content of a moral sentence does not consist in any moral proposition expressed, but rather in its use to express the noncognitive attitudes of the speaker:

Expressivism
The content of a moral sentence wholly consists in the noncognitive attitudes conveyed by its utterance.

These positive and negative claims are related. If there is nothing more to the content of a moral sentence than the noncognitive attitudes that its utterance conveys, and if these attitudes can be individuated independently of any moral property, then the content of a moral sentence cannot consist in any moral proposition expressed. So, from the fact, if it is one, that moral predicates have a nonrepresentational use, standard noncognitivists concluded that moral predicates have a nonrepresentational content. Moreover, if the content of at least the central attitude involved in moral acceptance is identical to the content of the accepted moral sentence, moral acceptance could not consist in belief in a moral proposition expressed by a moral sentence, for it expresses none.

Unfortunately, standard noncognitivism faces serious difficulties. In its most transparently noncognitivist form, an atomistic reduction of moral content to the expression of noncognitive attitudes, it faces an unanswerable dilemma. In a form that avoids this, the position is deprived of the means of demonstrating its nonfactualist and hence noncognitivist standing. This chapter will examine these difficulties.

The Dilemma

Frege appeals to embeddings in unasserted contexts to argue that we can express propositions without asserting them, and hence that we must distinguish the force with which we utter a sentence from the proposition it expresses. Consider the sentence:

Schmidt is the author of the incompleteness theorem.

This sentence can occur in unasserted contexts, such as:

If Schmidt is the author of the incompleteness theorem, then Gödel is a fraud.

Edgar believes that Schmidt is the author of the incompleteness theorem.

Is it true that Schmidt is the author of the incompleteness theorem?

It is not the case that Schmidt is the author of the incompleteness theorem.

'Schmidt is the author of the incompleteness theorem' is a sentence of English.

Notice that, if a competent speaker utters the conditional, e.g.:

If Schmidt is the author of the incompleteness theorem, then Gödel is a fraud

he does not thereby assert that Schmidt is the author of the incompleteness theorem. A competent speaker can, without irrationality or pragmatic incoherence, assert that, if Schmidt is the author of the incompleteness theorem, then Gödel is a fraud, while at the same time asserting that Gödel and not Schmidt is the author of the incompleteness theorem. The antecedent of a conditional is an unasserted context, since in uttering the conditional competent speakers do not thereby assert the proposition expressed in its antecedent. The consequent of a conditional is an unasserted context as well, since in uttering the conditional competent speakers do not thereby assert the proposition expressed in its consequent. After all, a competent speaker can, without irrationality or pragmatic incoherence, assert that, if Schmidt is the author of the incompleteness theorem, then Gödel is a fraud, while at the same time asserting that Gödel is no fraud. Similarly, in asserting that Edgar believes that Schmidt is the author of the incompleteness theorem, a competent speaker does not thereby assert that Schmidt is the author of the incompleteness theorem. We can, and regularly do, ascribe beliefs that we do not share. Thus, the complement of a belief ascription is also an unasserted context, since in asserting a belief ascription competent speakers do not thereby assert the proposition expressed by the 'that'-clause. Similarly, if a competent speaker asks whether Schmidt is the author of the incompleteness theorem, he does not thereby assert that Schmidt is the author of the incompleteness theorem. In many contexts, the point of asking such a question is connected to the fact that the speaker is not in a position to assert the proposition. (In many contexts, though not all. Consider a logic teacher asking this question of a delinquent student; in this context, the point of the question is to determine whether or not the student is in a position to assert the proposition.) Obviously, in denying that Schmidt is the author of the incompleteness theorem a competent speaker does not assert that Schmidt is the author of the incompleteness theorem. Less obviously, in asserting that 'Schmidt is the author of the incompleteness theorem' is a sentence of English, one does not assert the proposition expressed by the quoted sentence. After all, the proposition expressed by the sentence:

'Schmidt is the author of the incompleteness theorem' is a sentence of English is not about Schmidt or the incompleteness theorem, but rather has a linguistic subject matter.

Frege uses the observation that sentences can occur meaningfully in unasserted contexts to distinguish the force of an utterance (the action performed by uttering a sentence) from its content (the proposition expressed by the uttered sentence). Specifically, if it is possible for embedded and freestanding occurrences of a sentence to mean the same despite the fact that only the freestanding occurrence is asserted, then the meaning of these occurrences could not consist, even in part, in the linguistic action performed.

Frege draws a parallel distinction between the act of judgment (belief in a proposition) and the content of a judgment (the proposition believed). Thus, someone can believe that if Schmidt is the author of the incompleteness theorem then Gödel is a fraud, while believing neither that Schmidt is the author of the incompleteness theorem nor that Gödel is a fraud. So the attitude of believing is no part of the propositions embedded in the conditional belief. Frege maintains that this is a special case of a more general phenomenon—that one can entertain a proposition without believing it—and that this requires that belief in a proposition be distinct from the proposition believed.

The occurrence of moral sentences in unasserted contexts is the basis of a much discussed dilemma for expressivism first raised by David Ross (1939: 33–4) and independently by Peter Geach (1958, 1960, 1965) and John Searle (1962, 1969). Consider, for the sake of argument, the kind of primitive emotivism that A. J. Ayer advocated:

It is worth mentioning that ethical terms do not serve only to express feeling. They are calculated also to arouse feeling, and so to stimulate action. ... In fact we may define the meaning of the various ethical words in terms both of the different feelings they are ordinarily taken to express, and also the different responses which they are calculated to provoke. (Ayer, 1946: 108)

Suppose that, in uttering the freestanding sentence 'Lying is wrong,' a competent speaker does not so much represent lying as having the property of wrongness but rather expresses his disapproval of lying and provokes disapproval of lying in others. Unfortunately, occurrences of this sentence in unasserted contexts pose a problem for primitive expressivism. For the utterance of the sentence 'If lying is wrong, then getting one's little brother to lie is wrong' does not normally express any attitude of disapproval towards lying, nor does it normally provoke disapproval of lying in others. If the expressivist account applies to occurrences of sentences within unasserted contexts, then it falsely claims that the embedded sentence expresses the relevant noncognitive attitude.

The primitive expressivist would avoid this difficulty if he claimed that his account applies only to freestanding occurrences of moral sentences. However, if the account applies only to freestanding occurrences of moral sentences, then it is incomplete, for we would lack an account of their content in unasserted contexts. Furthermore, if the contents of freestanding and embedded occurrences of a moral sentence are differently determined, what guarantee is there that the differently determined contents are the same? The emotivist needs to provide some guarantee that freestanding and embedded occurrences of a moral sentence mean the same despite the fact that different factors determine their contents. For, if freestanding and embedded occurrences of moral sentences differ in content, then the emotivist is apparently committed to the invalidity of recognized forms of valid argument. Consider the following argument:

P1 If lying is wrong, then getting one's little brother to lie is wrong.

P2 Lying is wrong.

C Therefore, getting one's little brother to lie is wrong.

At first blush, this argument would appear to be just as valid as the following nonmoral argument:

P1 If Schmidt is the author of the incompleteness theorem, then Gödel is a fraud.

P2 Schmidt is the author of the incompleteness theorem.

C Therefore, Gödel is a fraud.

However, if the two occurrences of 'Lying is wrong' (in the major and minor premises) differ in content, then the argument is only apparently valid. Indeed, it would be an instance of the fallacy of equivocation.

Most critics focus on the primitive expressivist's apparent commitment to the invalidity of recognized forms of valid argument. However, there are other problems with the claim that embedded and freestanding occurrences of moral sentences differ in content. Thus, for example, if embedded and freestanding occurrences of moral sentences differ in content, then in uttering 'Bernice believes that lying is wrong' a competent speaker is not ascribing to Bernice the same 'belief' (or belief-like attitude) that she would convey by uttering 'Lying is wrong.' Furthermore, if embedded and freestanding occurrences of moral sentences differ in content, then, if a competent speaker were to ask whether lying is wrong, uttering 'Lying is wrong' would be no answer. The question and purported answer would differ in content and, hence, subject matter. Similarly, uttering 'It is not the case that lying is wrong' would not be to deny the utterance of 'Lying is wrong,' since the assertion and purported denial would themselves differ in content and, hence, subject matter.

Primitive expressivism faces the following dilemma:

The Dilemma
The primitive expressivist must claim either:

H1 that freestanding and embedded occurrences of a moral predicate have the same content, or

H2 that freestanding and embedded occurrences of a moral predicate differ in content.

However, H1 is apparently incompatible with the atomistic reduction of moral content to the expression of noncognitive attitudes; and H2 is apparently incompatible with the validity of moral arguments, the possibility of ascribing a moral belief conveyed by an utterance, the possibility of answering a moral question, the possibility of denying a moral claim, etc.

The dilemma is the result of the atomistic reduction of moral content to the expression of noncognitive attitudes. The primitive expressivist claims that the content of a moral predicate consists in its use to express the relevant noncognitive attitudes. However, sentences containing a moral predicate F have embedded and freestanding occurrences, and not every embedded occurrence expresses the relevant attitudes. But, if it is possible for embedded and freestanding occurrences of a sentences containing F to mean the same despite the fact that only freestanding occurrences express the relevant noncognitive attitudes, then it is hard to see how the content of these occurrences could consist, even in part, in the expression of such attitudes.

It is the identification of moral contents with the expression of noncognitive attitudes, and not the supervenience of moral content on the expression of such attitudes, that is responsible for the dilemma. Indeed, there is an alternative explanation of the supervenience of moral content on the expression of noncognitive attitudes that is not subject to the dilemma. Thus, for example, a moral realist might accept R. M. Hare's (1952) claim that freestanding attributions of goodness express commendation. He might even be a use theorist of meaning and accept that the content of 'good' supervenes on its commendatory use.

He might maintain as well that, in using the predicate 'good' to commend something, a competent speaker is, implicitly at least, describing something as commendable. Moreover, if he further maintains that something is commendable insofar as it is good, the description 'the property that makes something commendable' might plausibly be said to fix the denotation of the predicate 'good.' Conveying a noncognitive attitude by uttering a sentence containing a moral predicate might determine the predicate's content, at least in part, by implicitly defining its denotation. (This sketch of an account, though primitive, is sufficient for present purposes. For a sophisticated version of this kind of account see Wedgwood, 2001.)

Moreover, unlike the primitive expressivist, this hypothetical moral realist is not subject to the dilemma. Suppose the content of 'good' supervenes on its commendatory use. Whereas freestanding attributions of goodness normally commend things, embedded attributions of goodness do not. The challenge, then, is to say how freestanding and embedded occurrences can mean the same, given that the content of 'good' depends on its commendatory use in which the former but not the latter participates. The moral realist, however, in maintaining that 'good' is property denoting, can easily meet this challenge. The moral realist maintains that 'good' denotes goodness because freestanding attributions of goodness normally function to commend things. He further maintains that the content of 'good' is determined, at least in part, by its denoting goodness. However, there is no reason why he cannot maintain that occurrences of 'good' in unasserted contexts denote goodness as well and thus retain this content. Although 'good' comes to denote goodness by freestanding attributions of goodness normally functioning to commend things, 'good' can continue to denote goodness even in contexts where this commendatory function is suspended. The moral realist, in maintaining that moral predicates are property denoting, can specify a common element of meaning between freestanding and embedded occurrences of moral predicates and thus can avoid the charge of equivocation.

Notice that the primitive expressivist cannot say this. He maintains that moral content supervenes on the expression of noncognitive attitudes because the content of a moral predicate is just its use to express the relevant noncognitive attitudes where these can be individuated independently of any denoted moral property. And, if there is nothing more to the contents of moral predicates than the noncognitive attitudes they express, then the contents of moral predicates could not consist, even in part, in their denoting properties. Thus, the primitive expressivist cannot avoid the charge of equivocation by claiming that freestanding and embedded occurrences of moral predicates codenote some property. However, it is hard then to see how, according to primitive expressivism, there could be a common element of meaning between freestanding and embedded occurrences of moral predicates. If moral content is just the expression of noncognitive attitudes, and freestanding and embedded occurrences of moral predicates express distinct attitudes, then freestanding and embedded occurrences could not mean the same thing. The dilemma is the direct result of the particular way in which the primitive expressivist explains the supervenience of moral content on the expression of noncognitive attitudes, i.e. by an atomistic reduction of moral content to the expression of these attitudes.

'It's Everybody's Problem'

To underscore this, let's briefly look at a tempting reply to the dilemma that misses the point. The expressivist might seek to lessen his guilt by incriminating others. In ordinary representational discourse, the content of a sentence S is the belief expressed by its utterance. If that's right, then any account of representational discourse faces the same dilemma as the nonfactualist. For embedded occurrences of S do not express the belief that S. If embedded occurrences do not express the belief that S, then in what does their meaning consist? And if the contents of embedded occurrences of S are determined in some way other than by their expressing the belief that S, what guarantee do we have that the embedded and freestanding occurrences of S mean the same? We should be confident that there is some way of resolving the dilemma in accounting for representational discourse. Thus, we should be confident that the expressivist could simply retrofit that account in reformulating his expressivist semantics. The dilemma is not a problem peculiar to expressivist semantics. The dilemma is everybody's problem.

Alan Gibbard might be an example of an expressivist who has succumbed to this temptation:

Normative judgments, we can say, are to [basic normative attitudes] just as factual judgments are to factual apprehension.... Saying this, of course, leaves much to do: we now have to explain how judgment relates to apprehending. But this is equally work for the nonfactualist and the factualist. The expressivist who is challenged that he can't span the gap can reply: Show me how to do it in the factual realm, and I'll mimic you in the normative realm. (Gibbard, 1992: 971)

Simon Blackburn comes perilously close as well:

Suppose I say that the sentence 'Bears hibernate' expresses a belief. Well, it only does so when the sentence is put forward in an assertoric context. So what happens when it is put forward in an indirect context, such as 'If bears hibernate, then they wake up hungry'? For here no belief in bears hibernating is expressed. The standard answer is to introduce a proposition or thought, regarded as a constant factor in both the assertoric and the indirect context. When we say bears hibernate, we express or assert the proposition, and represent ourselves as believing it; when we say 'If bears hibernate ...' we introduce the proposition in a different way, conditionally, or as a supposition. Frege thought that in this second kind of context we refer to the thought that we assert in the assertoric context.

If this is allowed to solve the problem for ordinary beliefs, it might simply be taken over by the expressivist. In the Fregean story a 'proposition' or 'thought' is simply introduced as the common element between contexts: something capable of being believed but equally capable of being merely supposed or entertained. So why not say the same about an 'attitude'? (Blackburn, 1998: 71)

An answer to this latter question (not Blackburn's) will emerge in sequel.

The objection begins with the claim that in representational discourse the content of a sentence S is the belief expressed by its utterance, and concludes that the representationalist is subject to the same dilemma as the primitive expressivist. This line of reasoning goes wrong at the very first step. There is an ambiguity in our ordinary talk of belief. Sometimes by 'belief' we mean a kind of propositional attitude—a belief in a proposition. Sometimes by 'belief' we mean the object of that attitude—the proposition believed. (Compare this latter usage with Frege's use of 'thought.') It is not true that the content of a sentence is the belief that its utterance normally expresses, if by 'belief' we mean the propositional attitude of belief. The content of a sentence S is not belief in the proposition that S; rather, the content of S is simply the proposition that S (i.e. the proposition the utterance of S normally conveys belief in). The content of a (context insensitive) sentence is a proposition and not a belief in that proposition. This was Frege's point in distinguishing the act of judgment (belief in a proposition) from the content of a judgment (the proposition believed).

So the envisioned reply is undermined by an ambiguity in the initial assumption:

The content of a sentence S is the belief expressed by its utterance.

If 'belief' means the proposition that S, then the assumption is true, but the dilemma is not generated. (Embedded occurrences of S do express the proposition that S.) If 'belief' means belief in the proposition that S, then the dilemma is generated (embedded occurrences do not express the belief that S), but the assumption is false. The dilemma is not a general problem. It is a problem peculiar to expressivist semantics: the primitive expressivist denies that moral predicates are property denoting and so identifies moral content with the expression of noncognitive attitudes. And it is precisely this feature of his account that is responsible for the dilemma's apparent intractability.

The confusion of belief in a proposition with the proposition believed was facilitated by a further confusion—there is an ambiguity in our ordinary talk of expression and the present reply trades on it. Sometimes by 'express' we mean the semantic relation between a sentence and a proposition. Sometimes by 'express' we mean the pragmatic relation between an utterance of a sentence and an attitude—in this case, belief in a proposition. These relations differ not only in character—the former is semantic and the latter is pragmatic—but in relata as well—the former relates a sentence and a proposition, the latter an utterance and an attitude. We can regiment terminology as follows: 'express,' in the regimented sense, means the semantic relation between a sentence and a proposition, and 'convey,' in the regimented sense, means the pragmatic relation between the utterance and an attitude. Given our regimented terminology, we can say that the present reply conflates a sentence expressing a proposition with its utterance normally conveying belief in the proposition expressed. This is an instance of the pragmatic fallacy.

The Pragmatic Fallacy

The primitive expressivist is motivated by the observation that moral utterances have practical effects distinct from the assertion of a moral proposition. Specifically, the primitive expressivist maintains that, in sincerely uttering a moral sentence S, competent speakers who understand S express noncognitive attitudes that can be individuated independently of any denoted moral property. Thus, Ayer claims that attributions of wrongness normally convey disapproval and provoke disapproval in others. Recall that 'convey,' in our regimented sense, is a pragmatic relation between the utterance of a sentence and an attitude (in this case, disapproval and the provocation of disapproval). But the primitive expressivist claims more than this: he claims that the content of a moral predicate is just the property that utterances of sentences containing it normally convey some attitude distinct from belief in a moral proposition. Thus, Ayer claims that the meaning of 'wrong' is just the property that utterances of sentences containing it normally convey disapproval and provoke disapproval in others. The difficulty is, of course, that meaningful occurrences of 'wrong' in unasserted contexts lack this property. The primitive expressivist moves too quickly from the observation that moral utterances have practical effects to the claim that their content is nothing over and above these effects. The primitive expressivist is subject to the dilemma because, in identifying moral content with noncognitive attitudes normally conveyed, he has committed *the pragmatic fallacy*: the primitive expressivist mistakes the contents of moral sentences with what their utterances normally convey.

Here I am echoing John Dewey's criticism of Stevenson:

One can agree fully that ethical sentences (as far as their end and use is concerned) 'plead and advise' and speak 'to the conative-affective natures of men.' Their use and intent is practical. But the point at issue concerns the means by which this result is accomplished. It is . . . a radical fallacy to convert the end-in-view into an inherent constituent of the means by which, in genuinely moral sentences, the end is accomplished. To take the cases in which 'emotional' factors accompany the giving of reasons as if this accompaniment factor were an inherent part of the judgment is, I submit, both a theoretical error and is, when widely adopted in practice, a source of moral weakness. (Dewey, 1945: 702–3)

The end-in-view of moral utterance may be practical in the way the emotivist conceives, but one should not mistake this for its meaning, an inherent constituent of the means by which this end is accomplished. (Whether Dewey was right in maintaining that this mistake was a source of moral weakness will be discussed in Chapter 4.) Dewey further suggests that an ambiguity in our semantic vocabulary contributes to the commission of the pragmatic fallacy:

[Emotivists are] influenced at times in connection with the 'meaning' of moral judgments, by that ambiguity in which 'meaning' has the sense of both design or purpose and that which a sign indicates. (Dewey, 1945: 704)

The meaning of an uttered moral sentence in the sense of 'that which a sign indicates' is the moral proposition expressed by that sentence. The meaning of an uttered moral sentence in the sense of 'design or purpose' is what is meant by that utterance—what is communicated or otherwise conveyed by means of it in the context of utterance. 'Meaning' in the former sense is the proposition expressed by a sentence in the context of utterance. 'Meaning' in the latter sense is the attitude conveyed by its utterance in that context. The ambiguity is potentially influential in that it both makes possible and renders intelligible the pragmatic fallacy—that is, mistaking an attitude conveyed by a moral utterance for the meaning of the uttered moral sentence.

Expressivism, Primitive and Sophisticated

Not every philosopher accepts the pragmatic fallacy. Indeed, contemporary expressivists have in general offered various extensions of their respective brands of expressivism. Specifically, they grant that utterances of moral sentences that occur in unasserted contexts do not convey the attitudes that utterances of freestanding moral sentences convey. They grant as well that, if the content of a moral sentence simply consists in the attitudes conveyed by moral utterance, then seemingly valid arguments involving moral premises are in fact invalid (due to the fallacy of equivocation). They contend, however, that things are not so simple. Specifically, contemporary expressivists maintain that there is a way to extend their expressivist semantics so as to avoid this latter difficulty. Put another way, while the dilemma may be fatal for certain primitive forms of expressivism, there may be sophisticated forms of expressivism that are not subject to the dilemma.

We can get clearer on the gestured contrast between primitive and sophisticated expressivism if we recognize that the earliest forms of expressivist semantics—the explicit targets of Ross, Geach, and Searle—were forms of semantic behaviorism.

It is easy to see that Ayer's emotivism is a form of semantic behaviorism; for, according to Ayer, expressions and provocations of emotional attitudes are publicly observable intentional actions and the contents of moral predicates supervene on them. Indeed, all of the original targets of Ross, Geach, and Searle were forms of semantic behaviorism: they each explained the meanings of target sentences in terms of the linguistic behavior of competent speakers. Strawson's (1950) expressivist semantics for truth ascriptions explained the contents of a truth ascription in terms of the endorsement of the speaker. Carnap's (1997) expressivist semantics for moral discourse explained the contents of moral sentences in terms of the commands normally issued by uttering them, and so on.

If primitive expressivism is a kind of semantic behaviorism, sophisticated expressivism is a kind of functional role semantics. Thus, for example, Blackburn (1998: 77) glosses his present approach to moral semantics as 'nondescriptive functionalism' or 'practical functionalism.' Alan Gibbard's account of normative content is broadly functionalist as well:

Normative judgment gets its content through inferential ties: through the combinations of norm and fact it rules out, and through ties to experience and normative governance. (Gibbard, 1990: 105)

What is important here is that neither Blackburn nor Gibbard explains the contents of moral predicates in terms of the attitudes they are used to convey. In this way, they distance themselves from the semantic behaviorism of their nonfactualist predecessors. Rather, they explain the contents of moral predicates in terms of the functional role the acceptance of sentences containing them play in moral discourse and in the cognitive psychology of competent speakers.

In the previous section I suggested that, while the dilemma may be fatal for primitive expressivism, sophisticated nonfactualism might not be subject to the dilemma. We are now in a position to state clearly the gestured contrast. Whereas primitive expressivism is a kind of semantic behaviorism, sophisticated expressivism is a kind of functional role semantics. (In an insightful paper, Wedgwood, 2001, correctly observes, however, that a moral functional role semantics is not necessarily a form of nonfactualism—an observation that will be discussed in sequel.)

How Nonfactualist Is Sophisticated Expressivism?

Can this kind of functional role semantics sustain a nonfactualist interpretation of moral discourse? Recall that it was Ayer's explanation of the supervenience of moral content on the noncognitive attitudes conveyed that entailed that moral content is nonrepresentational. If there is nothing more to the content of a moral predicate than the noncognitive attitudes that it is used to convey and these attitudes can be individuated independently of any denoted property, then its content could not consist, even in part, in the denotation of a property. Sophisticated nonfactualism, in abandoning semantic behaviorism for functional role semantics, must accept the nonrepresentation thesis on other grounds. But it is not obviously entailed by a moral functional role semantics. If the functional role of a moral predicate is sufficiently complex, perhaps it imposes sufficient constraints on the predicate's content to determine a denotation. One worry about sophisticated expressivism, then, is whether it can vindicate its nonfactualist standing. If it cannot, then there is nothing particularly nonfactualist about sophisticated expressivism. Another worry is whether sophisticated expressivism can explain why the alleged determinants of moral content really are determinants of moral content, as opposed to features of moral acceptance and pragmatics. In the present instance, the challenge is to explain why the functional role of a moral predicate is semantically significant. I will press this challenge by showing how to reinterpret a sophisticated expressivist semantics as an account of moral acceptance and pragmatics.

Gibbard's Norm Expressivism

It will be useful to illustrate these worries by examining a particular version of sophisticated expressivism in detail. Gibbard's (1990) account of normative content will be our stalking horse.

There are two independent components to Gibbard's overall view. First, Gibbard is a rationalist, in the sense that he identifies the claims of morality with the claims of reason. Specifically, Gibbard understands moral claims as claims about the rationality of sentiment. Thus, for example, an action is wrong just in case it is rational to feel guilty for performing that action, and it is rational to be angry with a person that performs that action.

Second, Gibbard is a nonfactualist about rationality. In seemingly asserting that something is rational, a competent speaker is not ascribing a property to it but is rather expressing a psychological state—roughly, the acceptance of a system of norms that permits it (where *norms* are something like prescriptions or imperatives). Each component of the overall view is logically independent of the other. One could be a rationalist about morality and yet maintain that there are facts about reason; and one could be a nonfactualist about rationality and yet deny that the claims of morality are claims of reason. We will focus on the second, nonfactualist, component of Gibbard's account.

Gibbard presents his nonfactualism about rationality in two successive accounts. Interestingly, this is an instance of ontogeny recapitulating phylogeny: Whereas the preliminary account is a species of semantic behaviorism, the subsequent account is a species of functional role semantics.

Gibbard's preliminary account is this. To seemingly assert that something is rational is for a competent speaker to express his acceptance of a system of norms that permits it. Here, Gibbard is following Ayer's pattern of analysis: just as Ayer claims that the content of the predicate 'wrong' supervenes on the expression and provocation of disapproval, Gibbard claims that the content of the predicate 'rational' supervenes on the expression of the acceptance of a system of norms. Moreover, just as Ayer claims that the content of 'wrong' supervenes on the expression and provocation of disapproval because there is nothing more to the content of that predicate than the expression and provocation of disapproval, Gibbard claims that the content of 'rational' supervenes on the expression of the acceptance of a system of norms because there is nothing more to the content of that predicate than the expression of the acceptance of a system of norms. And since in each case there is nothing more to the contents of the relevant predicates than their use to convey the relevant attitudes, and these can be individuated independently of any denoted property, their contents could not consist, even in part, in the denotation of a property. It ought to be clear, then, that Gibbard's preliminary expressivist semantics, no less than Ayer's, is a kind of atomistic semantic behaviorism.

The problem, of course, is that Gibbard's preliminary account is subject to the same dilemma that Ayer's account is subject to, and precisely because it is a kind of atomistic semantic behaviorism. Indeed, this is one of the problems that explicitly motivates Gibbard's subsequent, more sophisticated account. The subsequent account has three components: a formal representation of the contents of normative sentences, a mapping of that formal representation onto the functional role of the acceptance of these sentences in normative discourse and in the cognitive psychology of competent speakers, and an independent argument that the represented contents are nonrepresentational.

Gibbard's formal representation is an extension of possible worlds semantics. In possible worlds semantics the content of a (context insensitive) sentence—'Bernice is fond of rabbits,' say— is the set of all possible worlds in which the denotation of 'Bernice' exists and instantiates the property denoted by 'is fond of rabbits.' According to Gibbard's nonfactualism, however, 'rational' is not property denoting, and so normative sentences do not determine sets of possible worlds. Gibbard's idea is to represent the contents of normative sentences as sets but not as sets of possible worlds. Suppose Edgar were to utter 'Optimism about the capital markets is rational.' The content of this sentence is represented by the set of all world–norm pairs, $<w, n>$, such that n is a complete system of norms that permits optimism about the capital markets in w. Worlds, here, are just possible worlds as they are ordinarily conceived, though by Gibbard's lights possible worlds do not involve the instantiation of normative properties, for he denies that there are any such properties. Norms, here, are prescriptions that certain things are permitted, forbidden, or obligatory, and a complete system of norms is such that, for every possible circumstance, it partitions the alternatives open to a person in that circumstance as permitted, forbidden, or obligatory. Just as sets of possible worlds can uniformly represent the contents of representational sentences in embedded and freestanding occurrences, the thought is that sets of world–norm pairs can uniformly represent the contents of normative sentences in freestanding and embedded occurrences, even though they are nonrepresentational. Given that the formalism can uniformly represent the contents of normative sentences in freestanding and embedded occurrences, Gibbard's norm expressivism might not seem to be subject to the dilemma in the way primitive expressivism is.

Though commentators have represented Gibbard's formalism as a solution to the dilemma (no doubt encouraged, somewhat, by Gibbard's own presentation of these matters), the formalism is not the whole solution—as Gibbard himself recognizes. After an initial presentation of the formalism, Gibbard (1990: 97) writes that 'embedded occurrences now pose no special problem,' but earlier he is more careful:

Roughly the normative content of a statement is the set of fully opinionated states one could be in and still accept the statement. Here I say almost nothing about what the representation might have to do with meaning, with what the person who accepts the statement has in mind. In the next section I go on to the second stage: saying how the representation helps in the theory of meaning. (Gibbard, 1990: 94)

The 'second stage' is the mapping of the formalism onto the functional role of normative acceptance.

The challenge posed by the dilemma is to specify some common element of meaning between freestanding and embedded occurrences of the target vocabulary. The primitive expressivist, in identifying nonrepresentational content with noncognitive attitudes conveyed, could not meet this challenge. So we need some other reason for thinking that nonrepresentational contents can be uniformly represented in freestanding and embedded occurrences. Put another way, we need some reason for thinking that the formalism can represent the contents of normative sentences *as the nonfactualist conceives of them*. Sets of world–norm pairs would uniformly represent the contents of normative sentences in freestanding and embedded occurrences. But the formalism does not by itself guarantee that the represented contents are nonrepresentational. Notice that, despite Gibbard's colorful talk of 'worlds' and 'norms,' there is nothing particularly nonfactualist about the formal representation: suitably understood, even a realist about rationality could accept it. Recall that, by Gibbard's lights, possible worlds do not involve the instantiation of normative properties, for he denies that there are any such properties. From the realist's perspective, however, possible worlds, as Gibbard conceives of them, are not possible worlds but descriptive cores of possible worlds—completely determinate ways the world might have been in every nonnormative respect. Moreover, the realist about rationality would maintain that norms are not (or are not merely) prescriptions that the speaker accepts but are responses to what reasons there are. If worlds and norms are understood as the realist might understand them, then there is nothing particularly nonfactualist about representing the contents of normative sentences as sets of world–norm pairs. The second component of Gibbard's account purports to provide a reason for thinking that sets of world–norm pairs represent normative contents, and the third component provides a reason for thinking that the represented contents are nonrepresentational.

The second component of Gibbard's account is a mapping of the formal representation onto the functional role of normative acceptance. Whereas, on the preliminary account, the content of 'rational' supervenes on attitude conveyed by uttering sentences containing it, on the subsequent account the meaning of 'rational' supervenes on the functional role of the acceptance of sentences containing it. Gibbard has an explanation of the supervenience of normative content on functional role: the content of a normative sentence S supervenes on the functional role of S's acceptance because a radical interpreter fully knowledgeable about that functional role could know S's content on that basis. (Gibbard, 1990, cites Davidson, 1984: essays 1, 2, 9–11, 13; but it is unclear to me whether, like Davidson, the interpreter is an ineliminable part of the explanation of the supervenience thesis, or whether, like Lewis, 1983, the interpreter is an eliminable heuristic for displaying how 'the facts determine the facts.') Moreover, the reason the relevant set O_S of world–norm pairs can represent the content of S is that a radical interpreter could interpret S by assigning O_S to it. States with sets of world–norm pairs as their contents have a distinctive kind of functional role: The functional role of such states include not only their role in perception and reasoning, but their role in action as well. Thus, not only would an interpreter assign O_S to S only if the pattern of entailments O_S participates in matches the speaker's reasoning in obvious ways; but, just as importantly, O_S should match the speaker's normative governance. Normative governance is a speaker's (not invariable) disposition to act in accordance with a norm that he accepts and is a component of a biologically adaptive, discursively mediated system of social cooperation. Suppose S is the sentence 'It is rational to take the bus to work.' If a competent speaker accepts S and is consequently disposed to take the bus to work, then O_S should include only those world–norms pairs $<w, n>$, where n permits taking the bus to work in w. It is this mapping of the formal representation onto the functional role of normative acceptance that vindicates its claim to represent the contents of normative sentences. And, since the formalism uniformly represents the contents of normative sentences in freestanding and embedded occurrences, it might seem, then, that Gibbard's sophisticated expressivism is not subject to the dilemma the way primitive expressivism is.

Gibbard's Case for Nonfactualism

Gibbard's sophisticated expressivism is a kind of functional role semantics. What makes it the case that normative sentences mean what they do is the functional role their acceptance plays in normative discourse and in the cognitive psychology of competent speakers. The mapping of the formal representation onto this functional role may vindicate its claim to represent the contents of normative sentences, but what guarantee is there that the represented contents are nonrepresentational? After all, the nonrepresentation thesis is no longer underwritten by an identification of normative content with the expression of noncognitive attitudes, so what reason is there to think that normative discourse is nonrepresentational? And, if the functional role of normative acceptance determines representational contents, then there is nothing particularly nonfactualist about Gibbard's norm expressivism.

Moreover, we need some reason to think that represented contents are nonrepresentational if Gibbard's account is a wholly adequate response to the dilemma. In order to successfully meet the challenge posed by the dilemma, the expressivist needs to provide some reason for thinking that the nonrepresentational contents can be uniformly represented in freestanding and embedded occurrences. The formalism would uniformly represent the contents of freestanding and embedded occurrences. (The same set of world–norm pairs would be assigned.) Moreover, the mapping of the formalism onto the functional role of normative acceptance is a reason to think that the formalism represents the contents of normative sentences. However, we so far lack a reason to think that the represented contents are nonrepresentational. We so far lack a reason to think that the formalism can represent the contents of normative sentences *as the nonfactualist conceives of them*. And until we do, Gibbard's response to the dilemma is incomplete. I do not mean this to be a criticism: Gibbard is aware of this explanatory debt and discharges it by providing an independent argument that the represented contents are nonrepresentational.

Begin with the linguistic distinction between normative and descriptive predicates. The distinction is intuitively obvious, at least in the sense that, over a wide range of cases, competent speakers can reliably classify predicates as normative or descriptive. The normative realist maintains that there is a metaphysical distinction corresponding to this linguistic distinction: just as there are normative and descriptive predicates, there are normative and descriptive properties. Nonfactualists, in contrast, deny that there are any normative properties. In this dispute between the realist and the nonfactualist, how are we to decide what kind of property normative properties would be if indeed there were any? As the linguistic distinction is common ground between the realist and the nonfactualist, we might begin with it and see if the metaphysical distinction could be explained in terms of it. Maybe a property is normative because it is denoted by a normative predicate. The normative realist and nonfactualist might then agree at least to this extent: normative properties, if there were any, would be the denotations of normative predicates.

The nonfactualist could then argue for the nonrepresentation thesis as follows. What makes a predicate normative is its distinctive use—the functional role that the acceptance of sentences containing it play in normative discourse and the cognitive psychology of competent speakers. But if the functional role of normative predicates can be explained without supposing that they denote any distinctively normative properties, then what reason is there to suppose that they denote such properties? And if normative predicates were nondenoting, then there would be no normative properties (since normative properties would just be the properties picked out as the denotations of normative predicates). Normative predicates are nondenoting because their denoting normative properties is unnecessary to explain the acceptance of sentences containing them. Gibbard's case takes precisely this form:

In the end, to be sure, I do deny that there are normative facts—but only in the end. Normative facts, if there were any, would be the facts of the special kind represented, naturally or artificially, by normative judgments. That is what would pick them out as normative. As it turns out, I claimed, our making these judgments can be explained without supposing they represent facts of any special kind. Thus at the end of the argument we can conclude that, at least in this sense, there are no normative facts. (Gibbard, 1990: 122)

This is an instance of a familiar argument for moral irrealism (see Harman, 1977; Harman and Thompson, 1996; Sturgeon, 1988).

There are a number of ways to resist this argument, but let me focus on two.

Even assuming the truth of its premises, one might worry that Gibbard's argument proves too much. It is distinctive of functional role semantics quite generally that the content of a target predicate is explained in terms of its functional role. According to functional role semantics, a predicate does not have the functional role it does because of what it means: rather, it means what it does because of its functional role. Moreover, the functional role of a predicate is specified independently of the property it denotes, if any. So, where the content of a predicate allegedly consists, at least in part, in the property it denotes, the content of the predicate is explained without supposing that it is property denoting. So if Gibbard's argument is consistently applied, every version of functional role semantics is a version of nonfactualism. But that is implausible. It is not obviously inconsistent to believe that the target predicates are representational and that their contents are determined by their functional roles, but if Gibbard's argument were correct it would be obvious. (This point will be elaborated in the next section.)

It is conceivable, then, that the functional role of normative acceptance places sufficient constraints on the content of a normative predicate to determine a denotation for it. Consider the predicate 'rational.' This predicate is applicable to an action in a given circumstance just in case there is a world–norm pair consistent with everything the speaker accepts that permits that action in that circumstance. What is it for a system of norms to permit an action in a given circumstance? If the normative standard takes the form of permitting actions with a certain property in the given circumstance, then a case can be made for 'rational' being property denoting.

On the present understanding, a complete system of norms will determine, for every possible circumstance, that actions with a certain property in that circumstance are permissible. Perhaps it is the same property in every circumstance (the maximization of expected utility, say), or perhaps in different circumstances actions with different properties will be permissible. In the latter case, there will nevertheless be a complex property that might serve as the denotation of 'rational': the property such that in circumstance c actions with p are permissible, and in circumstance c^* actions with p^* are permissible, and in circumstance c^{**} actions with p^{**} are permissible, and so on. In either case, the functional role of normative acceptance will determine a property associated with the predicate 'rational.'

While the functional role of a normative predicate might determine a property associated with it, this is not yet to establish that the content of the predicate consists, even in part, in the denotation of that property. Indeed, Gibbard (1990: 118) claims that, even if there were such a property associated with the use of a normative predicate, a variant of the open question argument suffices to show that it is not the denotation of that predicate. Let p be the (possibly complex) property determined by the functional role of the normative predicate F. A competent speaker might believe that an action has p in a given circumstance but lack the relevant disposition to act. Since a competent speaker can attribute p to an act and not be normatively governed by that attribution, the meaning of F does not consist in its denoting p. If the variant of the open question argument is sound, then, even if the functional role of a normative predicate determines an associated property, the determined property is not the denotation of that predicate. Unfortunately, the open question argument in its present form is unsound. Compare: A competent speaker may believe that a liquid sample is an aggregate of H_2O molecules and not be disposed to drink it (perhaps because he falsely believes that H_2O is not potable), but that does not establish that water is not an aggregate of H_2O molecules in a liquid state. So why should we conclude on parallel grounds that property p is not F-ness, i.e. the property denoted by F?

For all that has been said, normative discourse might be representational: normative predicates might denote normative properties even though normative properties are dispensable in explaining the acceptance of sentences containing them.

There is a second set of reasons to doubt the validity of Gibbard's argument. Gibbard reasons from the dispensability of normative properties in explaining the use of normative predicates to their being nonrepresentational: normative predicates are nondenoting because their denoting normative properties is unnecessary to explain the acceptance of sentences containing them. While the indispensability of normative properties might be a reason to believe that normative discourse is representational, it is controversial whether their dispensability is, by itself, a sufficient reason to believe that normative discourse is nonrepresentational. Suppose the nonnormative explanation is compatible with an alternative, empirically equivalent explanation of normative acceptance involving normative properties; then *at best* it would be rationally permissible to believe that normative discourse is nonrepresentational. But it would also be rationally permissible to believe that normative discourse is representational, and so the argument for the non-representation thesis would fail.

I will not rehearse all of the familiar doubts about indispensability arguments (see, *inter alia*, Burgess and Rosen, 1998; Field, 1980, 1989; van Fraassen, 1980). It suffices to question whether the functional role of normative predicates is semantically significant in the way that Gibbard claims it to be. One can agree that the acceptance of a normative sentence is a state whose content can be represented by Gibbard's formalism (as he understands it), and that in uttering a normative sentence the content conveyed can be similarly represented. One can even agree with Gibbard's explanation of normative acceptance and utterance as a biologically adaptive solution to a coordination problem. One can agree that a speaker's acceptance and utterance of normative sentences can be explained without supposing that normative properties exist, but that is nonetheless consistent with the denial of non-factualism. Normative predicates may denote moral properties, but they might not be used to represent the existence and distribution of normative properties, but instead to express the relevant noncognitive attitude.

Compare the resulting position with constructive empiricism: The fictionalist about science maintains that the acceptance and utterance of scientific theories can be explained without supposing anything about the nature or existence of unobservable structures, but he claims nonetheless that scientific theories purport to represent such structures. Similarly, the normative fictionalist maintains that the acceptance and utterance of a normative sentence can be explained without supposing anything about the nature or existence of normative facts, but he claims nonetheless that normative sentences purport to represent such facts. Since one can accept the truth of Gibbard's premises while consistently denying his conclusion, Gibbard's argument is invalid. Notice that, according to the envisioned position, the functional role that Gibbard assigns a normative predicate does not determine its content; rather, the assigned functional role is an account of the acceptance and utterance of sentences containing that predicate. According to this view, then, Gibbard's account is a better account of normative acceptance and pragmatics than of the determinants of normative semantics.

I presented two different worries about Gibbard's account. The first worry was this. Suppose that the functional role of normative predicates does indeed determine their content. The assigned functional role might place sufficient constraints on a normative predicate's content to determine a denotation. Indeed, Gibbard's account, suitably developed, is a representational moral functional role semantics. The second worry was this. Suppose that normative predicates have the functional role that Gibbard assigns them. The assigned functional role might be a better account of normative acceptance and pragmatics than of the determinants of normative semantics. These developments pull in different directions. The first concedes that the assigned functional role is semantically significant but claims that the determined content is representational. The second denies that the assigned functional role is semantically significant after all. That Gibbard's sophisticated expressivism is subject to incompatible developments is an echo of the pragmatic fallacy that beset its primitive predecessor.

Recall the diagnosis of the dilemma for primitive expressivism: the primitive expressivist conflates the contents of normative sentences with what their utterance normally conveys. Suppose that primitive expressivist were further developed in full recognition of this conflation. A coherent account, one not subject to the operative conflation, might develop along one of two lines. An account might be given of the contents of normative utterances, but a nonfactualist interpretation could not then be underwritten by an atomistic explanation of the supervenience of moral content on linguistic behavior. But then it would be an open question whether nonfactualism could be underwritten by some other means. Alternatively, an account might be given of the action normally performed by normative utterances. But then no account would be given of their content. Gibbard's sophisticated expressivism is subject to incompatible developments because it confusedly vacillates between these alternatives, thus echoing the pragmatic fallacy that beset its primitive predecessor. Moreover, I suspect that the same is true of any version of sophisticated expressivism.

Sophisticated Expressivism and the Pragmatic Fallacy

Can this more general claim be substantiated?

Sophisticated expressivists maintain that the content of a moral predicate is determined by its functional role in moral discourse and the cognitive psychology of competent speakers, and that the determined content is nonrepresentational. Suppose we grant, for the sake of argument, that the content of a moral predicate is determined by its functional role: why would the functional role of a moral predicate determine a nonrepresentational content for it? Why think that the determined content is nonrepresentational? Here are three candidate arguments:

Identification

The content of a moral predicate could not consist, even in part, in the denotation of a moral property because there is nothing more to the content of a moral predicate than the role it plays in moral discourse and in the cognitive psychology of competent speakers, and that role can be individuated independently of any denoted property. Moral predicates are nondenoting because their contents are identified with their functional roles.

Dispensability

The content of a moral predicate could not consist, even in part, in the denotation of a moral property because their denoting moral properties is unnecessary to explain the use of such predicates. The content of a moral predicate is explained not in terms of any denoted moral property, but rather in terms of the role it plays in moral discourse and in the cognitive psychology of competent speakers where that role can be individuated independently of any denoted moral property. Moral predicates are nondenoting because their denoting moral properties is unnecessary to explain the acceptance of sentences containing them.

Practical Function

The content of a moral predicate could not consist, even in part, in the denotation of a moral property, because of its practical function. The content-determining functional role of moral predicates involves relations to action in a way that the functional role of representational predicates do not. Moral predicates are nondenoting because of their practical function.

Let's consider these in turn.

Identification. Sophisticated expressivists, in abandoning the semantic behaviorism of their nonfactualist predecessors, could not identify the content of a moral predicate with the action that it is normally used to perform, but this is not to say that they could not endorse a substantive identification of their own. If there is nothing more to the content of a moral predicate than the role it plays in moral discourse and the cognitive psychology of competent speakers, and this role can be individuated independently of any denoted moral property, then its content could not consist, even in part, in the denotation of a moral property. The identification of the content of a moral predicate with its functional role can seem plausible: After all, doesn't a moral predicate's use *suffice* for its meaning? This is a mistake that results from conflating two thoughts. The functional role of a moral predicate certainly suffices for meaning what it does in the sense that the functional role of the predicate determines its content, but more is being claimed: the content of a moral predicate supervenes on the role it plays because its content just is that functional role. While we may be granting, for the sake of argument, the supervenience of moral content on functional role, one is not entitled to explain this in terms of the identification of moral content with functional role without further argument. After all, whereas the identification of the content of a moral predicate with its functional role may explain the supervenience of the former on the latter, there are alternative explanations. (We have already seen Gibbard provide one alternative explanation: that the content of a normative predicate supervenes on its functional role not because there is nothing more to its content than that functional role, but because an ideal interpreter fully knowledgeable of that role could know the content of the normative predicate on that basis.) Whereas the identification of moral content with functional role entails the supervenience of the former on the latter, the converse entailment fails.

Dispensability. Perhaps the identification of the content of a moral predicate with its functional role can be understood as the hyperbolic expression of a weaker claim: if the content of a moral predicate is just the role it plays in moral discourse and in the cognitive psychology of competent speakers, and this role can be individuated independently of any denoted moral property, then moral properties are semantically dispensable: they are unnecessary to explain the contents of moral predicates. Perhaps it is the semantic dispensability of moral properties, and not any controversial identification, that suffices for moral predicates to be nonrepresentational. The semantic dispensability of moral properties is a common theme among sophisticated expressivists. We have already seen Gibbard's attempt to establish the nonrepresentation thesis on the basis of semantic dispensability. Blackburn (1998: 77) endorses a similar line of thought: 'that the moral proposition [is] a "propositional reflection" of states that are first understood in other terms than that they represent anything . . . remains the core claim.'

We have seen that the argument from semantic dispensability proves too much: it entails that every version of functional role semantics is a version of nonfactualism. According to functional role semantics, a predicate does not have the functional role it has because of what it means: rather, it means what it does because of its functional role. Moreover, the functional role is specified independently of the property it denotes, if any. So, in the case where the content of a predicate allegedly consists, at least in part, in the property it denotes, the content of the predicate is explained without supposing that it is property denoting. However, if the content of the predicate can be explained without supposing that it is property denoting, then, if the argument from semantic dispensability is sound, every predicate whose content is explained by its functional role is nonrepresentational; but that is implausible.

Consider the most favorable case for functional role semantics—an inferential role semantics for logical discourse. It is not obviously inconsistent to believe that logical discourse is representational and that logical content is determined by inferential role. To suppose that logical discourse is representational is to suppose that logical vocabulary denotes logical objects—truth functions, quantifiers and the like. According to an inferential role semantics, the content of logical vocabulary is determined by its inferential role—roughly, the disposition of competent speakers to accept the validity of a distinguished set of inferences containing that vocabulary. Thus, the content of the material conditional might be determined, at least in part, by speakers' disposition to accept the validity of modus ponens. But in this way the material conditional might come to denote the relevant truth function, i.e. the truth function that would make the distinguished set of inferences valid. Moreover, an inferential role semantics seems like the only plausible semantics for such a platonist construal of logical discourse. Logical objects are abstract and exist necessarily if they exist at all, but this would seem to preclude their explaining the concrete and contingent use of logical vocabulary. So if logical vocabulary denotes logical objects, then it would seem that the only way they could is by having the inferential role they do—by the inferential role of logical vocabulary explaining their denotation of logical objects (see Kalderon, 2001).

The mere fact that no denotation is required to explain an expression's use does not establish that the expression lacks any such denotation. So the mere fact, if it is one, that no denoted moral property is required to explain the use of a moral predicate does not establish that the predicate lacks any such denotation.

Practical function. Perhaps it is not just the semantic dispensability of moral properties that necessitates a nonrepresentational semantics for moral discourse. Perhaps a nonfactualist interpretation is entailed by the semantic dispensability of moral properties in conjunction with a claim about the nature of the *explanans.* What is it about the nature of the functional role of moral predicates that determines a nonrepresentational content for them? A nearly irresistible thought is that it is the practical role of moral predicates that determines a nonrepresentational content for them. (Indeed, this is plausibly the thought behind Gibbard's deployment of the open question argument; see Darwall *et al.*'s 1992, interpretation of the open question argument.) It is because the content of a moral predicate is partly explained by the role it plays in the production of action that no moral property is denoted by that predicate. The functional role of moral predicates have the 'wrong direction of fit' to be representational. Thus, standard noncognitivists reason from the nonrepresentational role that the acceptance of sentences containing moral predicates play to moral predicates' having a nonrepresentational content.

That the acceptance of a moral sentence plays a distinctively practical role, that moral acceptance involves a motivation to act, is a common observation among noncognitivists. For example, it figures prominently in familiar internalist arguments for noncognitivism: moral acceptance motivates a person to act in a way that belief does not, so moral acceptance is some attitude other than belief in a moral proposition. Whether or not such arguments succeed, nonfactualists might exploit this observation in an argument for the nonrepresentation thesis: the functional role of a moral predicate involves relations to action in a way that the functional role of a representational predicate does not. Thus, Blackburn (1998: 77) glosses his present version of nonfactualism as both 'nondescriptive functionalism' and 'practical functionalism.' That Blackburn's expressivism is a kind of *practical* functionalism suggests that the content of a moral predicate is determined in part by its role in the production of action. That Blackburn's nonfactualism is a kind of *nondescriptive* functionalism suggests that the functional role of a moral predicate determines a nonrepresentational content for it. That Blackburn apparently regards these as equivalent suggests that he sees a connection between the practical function of a moral predicate and that predicate's being nonrepresentational.

Why would the practical function of a moral predicate determine a nonrepresentational content for it? What is it about the distinctively practical role that moral predicates play that rules out their being property-denoting?

One thought might be this. Whereas the content of representational predicates is determined by their functional role in perception and reasoning, the content of moral predicates is determined by their functional role in perception, reasoning, and action. Action is implicated in the functional role of moral predicates in a way that it is not in genuinely representational discourse, and this suffices to show that moral discourse is nonrepresentational.

This argument, however, is far too quick. It has the form—moral predicates have a feature—that representational predicates lack, and hence moral predicates are not representational predicates:

P1 The content-determining functional role of moral predicates involves relations to action.

P2 The content-determining functional role of representational predicates involves no relations to action.

C Moral predicates are not representational.

What is meant by 'representational predicates' in the second premise? On the one hand, it could mean uncontroversially representational predicates—paradigm exemplars of property denoting predicates. On the other hand, it could mean representational predicates full stop—all property denoting predicates, whether they are paradigm exemplars or not. This ambiguity is the basis of a dilemma. Suppose that representational predicates are understood as paradigm exemplars of property denoting predicates; then moral predicates would have a feature that paradigm exemplars of representational predicates lack. However, from this it does not follow that moral predicates are nonrepresentational, only that they are not paradigm exemplars of representational predicates. So understood, the argument is invalid due to the fallacy of equivocation. Suppose, however, that representational predicates are understood as property denoting predicates whether they are paradigm exemplars or not. Then moral predicates would have a feature that all representational predicates lack. But this assumes at the outset that moral predicates are not representational, which is what the argument is supposed to establish. So understood, the argument is question begging. Thus, the plausibility of the argument depends on confusedly vacillating between these two senses of 'representational.'

Moreover, if 'representational predicates' means all property denoting predicates whether they are paradigm exemplars or not, then the second premise—that the content determining functional role of representational predicates involves no relations to action—is plausibly false. That the content of a representational predicate is never determined by its role in the production of action may fairly be questioned. Thus, in standard Bayesian decision theory, belief states are individuated by their relation to action via a fine-grained Humean psychology. Moreover, Gibbard argues as follows:

Indeed in simple systems we can imagine states that act both as natural representations and as connations. Think of a housefly at rest. It flies off at the slightest sudden movement in its vicinity. That might well be due to [a] single state that both responds to sudden movement and elicits immediate flight. We could describe it as a natural connation to fly away: a mechanism that has the biological function of producing flight when activated. It is also, though, a natural representation of sudden movement in the vicinity: the mechanism that produces it has the biological function of making activation of the state correspond with sudden movement in the vicinity. (Gibbard, 1990: 110–11)

If a state can at once be a representation and a motivation to act, then there is no reason to doubt that a predicate could be representational and that its content could be determined in part by its role in the production of action.

The thought that the practical role that moral predicates play necessitates a nonrepresentational semantics for moral discourse is plausibly the result of conflating noncognitivism with nonfactualism. Noncognitivism is primarily a claim about moral acceptance—that the acceptance of a moral sentence is not belief in a moral proposition. Nonfactualism, in contrast, is primarily a claim about moral semantics—that moral sentences do not express moral propositions. That accepting a sentence containing a moral predicate can motivate a person to act in the way that belief does not may establish, if it does, that moral acceptance is some attitude other than moral belief, but it does not establish that moral sentences do not express moral propositions. The acceptance of a moral sentence may be some attitude other than belief in a moral proposition, but it does not follow that the accepted moral sentence fails to express a moral proposition. The confusion of noncognitivism with nonfactualism is facilitated by an ambiguity in our ordinary talk of belief. Recall that sometimes by 'belief' we mean a kind of propositional attitude—a belief in a proposition; sometimes by 'belief' we mean the object of that propositional attitude—the proposition believed. The practical role of moral acceptance may establish that moral acceptance is not belief understood as belief in a moral proposition, but it does not establish that the accepted moral sentence fails to express a moral proposition. To suppose otherwise is to confuse the propositional attitude of belief with the proposition allegedly believed. Indeed, this confusion is central to the nonfactualist's deployment of the 'direction of fit' metaphor: the fact that the functional role of moral acceptance has the 'wrong direction of fit' may establish that moral acceptance is not belief in a proposition, but it does not establish that the accepted sentence fails to express a moral proposition, a proposition that attributes moral properties to things.

As Dewey (1945) anticipated, a related ambiguity in our representational idiom may be relevant. The practical role that moral predicates play might be glossed as a nonrepresentational role. From this it is a short step to concluding that the practical role that moral predicates play necessitates a nonrepresentational semantics for them. Unfortunately, this conflates two senses of 'represent.' Sometimes by 'representing o as F' we mean that the proposition that o is F is being put forward as true. Sometimes by 'representing o as F' we mean that the proposition that o is F is expressed whether or not that proposition is being put forward as true. In the former sense, a representation is being put forward as true; in the latter sense, the content of a representation is being specified whether or not that representation is put forward as true. So consider the following utterance: 'Bernice's remark represents Edgar in a bad light.' The speaker might be making a claim about what Bernice's remark asserted—what it put forward as true—or the speaker might be making a claim about the content of the remark whether or not it was asserted— whether or not it was put forward as true. (Bernice might have been joking, or sarcastic, and so might not have been asserting the content of the remark—a fact that could be mutually known to speaker and hearer and one that would not undermine the appropriateness of the utterance.) That moral predicates have a practical function might entail, if it does, that moral predicates play a nonrepresentational role—but only in the sense that sentences containing moral predicates are not being put forward as true. But this is perfectly consistent with moral predicates being representational in the sense of denoting moral properties. Blackburn's claim that moral propositions are the propositional reflection of states that are first understood in other terms than that they represent anything might be plausible if such states did not represent anything in the sense of putting forward what they represent as true. But to conclude from this that the accepted moral sentence is nonrepresentational in the sense of not ex- pressing a moral proposition is to conflate distinct senses of 'represent.'

These considerations reveal the fundamental mistake under- lying the thought that the practical function of moral predicates necessitates a nonrepresentational semantics. It assumes that the use of a representation is invariably cognitive. If the use of a representation is invariably cognitive, then the discovery that the use of moral predicates is noncognitive suffices to establish that they are not representations. However, it is just not true that the use of a representation is invariably cognitive. A central cognitive use of a representation is to put forward that representation as true. While a representation might be used in that way, it need not. A representation can be used in all sorts of ways. Using it to claim that the world is the way the representation represents it to be is but one of them. Indeed, this is an important insight of Wittgenstein's:

But how many kinds of sentences are there? Say assertion, question, and command?—There are *countless* kinds: countless different kinds of use of what we call 'symbols', 'words', 'sentences'.... Review the multiplicity of language-games in the following examples, and in others:

Giving orders, and obeying them—

Describing the appearance of an object, or giving its measurements—

Constructing an object from a description (a drawing)—

Reporting an event—

Speculating about an event—

Forming and testing a hypothesis—

Presenting the results of an experiment in tables and diagrams—

Making up a story; and reading it—

Play-acting—

Singing catches—

Guessing riddles—

Making a joke; and telling it—

Solving a problem in practical arithmetic—

Translating from one language into another—

Asking, thanking, cursing, greeting, praying. (Wittgenstein, 1958: section 23)

In making up a story and reading it one does not put forward the story as true, but it remains a representation nonetheless. The same is true of making a joke and telling it. The same is true of utterances made while play-acting. The same is true of cursing, praying, and—plausibly—making a moral utterance. So the fact that moral sentences have a noncognitive use does not mean that they are not representations, that they do not express moral propositions. To suppose otherwise is to commit the pragmatic fallacy, broadly conceived, for it involves mistaking the use of a representation for what it represents.

While the dilemma posed by Ross, Geach, and Searle may be fatal for primitive expressivism, I wondered whether a sophisticated expressivism might not be subject to it. However, I have failed to discover, suitable grounds for a nonfactualist interpretation of moral discourse, even granting the kind of functional role semantics favored by sophisticated expressivists: identification is under-motivated, dispensability is insufficient, and practical function plausibly turns on the pragmatic fallacy.

Conclusion

Noncognitivism, in its primary sense, is a claim about moral acceptance. However, as standardly developed, it is a part of a syndrome of ideas that include negative and positive claims about moral semantics. Standard noncognitivists are nonfactualists in that they deny that the content of a moral sentence is a moral proposition. Standard noncognitivists are expressivists in that they claim that the content of a moral sentence is its use to express a noncognitive attitude. Standard noncognitivism faces serious difficulties. In its most transparently noncognitivist form, an atomistic reduction of moral content to the expression of noncognitive attitudes, it faces an unanswerable dilemma. In a form that avoids this, the position is deprived of the means of demonstrating its nonfactualist and hence noncognitivist standing. If the arguments for noncognitivism are compelling, we face a puzzle at this point: We appear to be in the uncomfortable position of choosing between a plausible semantics wedded to an implausible cognitivism and an implausible semantics wedded to a plausible noncognitivism. This puzzle would be resolved if there were forms of noncognitivism that are not nonfactualist. Demonstrating that there are forms of noncognitivism that eschew nonfactualism is the task of the following chapter.

3

Varieties of Moral Irrealism

Introduction

AN important obstacle to standard noncognitivism has been its apparent commitment to an implausible expressivist form of nonfactualism. However, noncognitivism—the claim that moral acceptance is some attitude other than belief—is not the exclusive province of nonfactualism. A novel alternative to moral realism, moral fictionalism, can vindicate noncognitivism as well and can do so without claiming that moral sentences are nonrepresentational. And if the problems for an expressivist nonfactualism prove intractable, then an adequate defense of noncognitivism necessarily involves the development of moral fictionalism. This involves rethinking the standard taxonomy of alternatives to moral realism.

The Standard Conception

It is remarkable that the current debate about moral realism is, to a large extent, framed as a debate about moral language. The label suggests that the proper topic of the debate is the reality of distinctively moral facts. Indeed, one might naively expect a frank discussion of questions of the form: Are there moral properties (such as rightness and wrongness), and if so are they actually instantiated? Are there moral facts, and if so what are their nature? But the standard formulation of these issues makes essential reference to linguistic intermediaries. The standard discussion of moral realism does not directly speak of moral facts; rather, it is framed in terms of moral sentences and whether they are used to express propositions that represent putative moral facts. Similarly, the existence and instantiation of moral properties are not directly discussed, but there is an extensive discussion of the proper use of moral predicates—whether or not they are normally used to denote moral properties and, if they are, whether they are true of anything in the actual world. It is at least unobvious how a discussion of moral discourse would bear on the metaphysics of morals. After all, the metaphysical commitments of a person as embodied in his use of language is one thing and reality is quite another. The extent to which the debate about moral realism is framed in terms of moral discourse suggests that, despite initial appearances, the debate is not primarily about the metaphysics of morals. Rather, moral realism is an epistemological posture or stance that is articulated, in part, in terms of the commitments embodied in our use of moral language. Specifically, according to a moral realist, he is justified in believing the propositions expressed by at least some of the moral sentences that he in fact accepts. So understood, the varieties of moral irrealism are special forms of moral skepticism. Or so I will argue.

The realist's epistemic stance is easy to characterize at least to a first approximation. In general, a realist about some topic regards thought and talk of the putative subject matter as representing a genuine domain of fact. To be a moral realist, then, is to understand moral thought and talk as representing a genuine domain of moral fact. But what exactly does this mean? One way to articulate the commitments of moral realism is to canvass the potential alternatives to it. This strategy is available because each of the alternatives to moral realism denies some necessary condition for being a moral realist. A complete taxonomy of the alternatives to moral realism will specify conditions that are individually necessary and jointly sufficient for being a moral realist. Thus, it is important to recognize all the potential forms of opposition if only to clarify the necessary and sufficient conditions for being a moral realist. As it stands, mainstream metaethics recognizes two varieties of moral irrealism: nonfactualism and the error theory. The nonfactualist and the error theorist each deny some necessary condition for being a moral realist. I will argue, however, that a further condition must be fulfilled in order for moral realism to be sustained. Moral fictionalism is the denial of precisely this condition.

To clarify the necessary and sufficient conditions for being a moral realist, I will begin by reviewing the recognized alternatives to moral realism.

The nonfactualist denies that moral sentences purport to represent moral reality, to say how things stand with the moral facts. Given our assumption that moral vocabulary consists solely in a class of predicates, we can usefully understand the moral nonfactualist as claiming that the content of a moral predicate does not consist in denoting a moral property:

> *The Nonrepresentation Thesis*
> The content of a moral predicate F does not consist in F denoting a moral property.

Sometimes the nonfactualist thesis is glossed by the slogan that moral sentences are incapable of truth or falsity. This slogan is potentially misleading—after all, even Ayer (1946) did not claim that moral utterances were utterly devoid of 'factual content.' Given the present framework, the slogan can be unpacked as follows. According to the nonrepresentation thesis, moral predicates do not denote moral properties. It is plausible to assume that the content of a complex expression is determined by the content of its constituent expressions—that some version of compositionality is true. The nonrepresentation thesis in conjunction with compositionality implies that the content of a moral sentence does not consist in its expressing a moral proposition (a proposition that attributes moral properties to things). And if no moral proposition is expressed, nothing, or at least nothing moral, is being put forward as true in uttering a moral sentence. Insofar as moral sentences are true or false, their truth-value does not depend on the instantiation of any moral property, for none are denoted. As such, moral sentences do not represent moral facts, facts about the existence and distribution of moral properties.

It is worth pointing out some consequences of the nonrepresentation thesis. The nonrepresentation thesis in conjunction with compositionality implies that the content of a moral sentence does not consist in its expressing a moral proposition. However, if belief is a relation between a believer and a proposition, the acceptance of a moral sentence cannot be belief in the moral proposition expressed, for it expresses none. Specifically, the nonfactualist is committed to the following:

> *The Noncognitive Thesis*
> In accepting a moral sentence S, competent speakers who understand S do not believe a moral proposition expressed by S.

Thus, according to emotivists, the acceptance of a moral sentence is not belief in a moral proposition expressed, for it expresses none but the adoption of the relevant emotional attitude. Similarly, according to prescriptivists, the acceptance of a moral sentence is not belief in a moral proposition expressed, for it expresses none but the intention to conform to the relevant prescription.

Just as the nonrepresentation thesis in conjunction with certain plausible assumptions implies that the acceptance of a moral sentence cannot be belief in a moral proposition expressed, it implies as well that the utterance of the moral sentence cannot be the assertion of a moral proposition expressed. Specifically, the nonrepresentation thesis in conjunction with compositionality implies that the content of a moral sentence does not consist in its expressing a moral proposition. However, if assertion is a relation between a speaker and a proposition, the utterance of a moral sentence cannot be the assertion of a moral proposition expressed, for it expresses none. Specifically, the nonfactualist is committed to the following:

> *The Nonassertion Thesis*
> In uttering a moral sentence S, competent speakers who understand S do not assert a moral proposition expressed by S.

Though advanced mainly in moral philosophy, nonfactualist theses have been advanced elsewhere as well. In the philosophy of mathematics, for example, there is a traditional interpretation of Wittgenstein where the formulas of pure arithmetic do not express mathematical propositions (propositions that represent the existence, properties, and relations of mathematical objects) but rather are prescriptions for the use of number words in counting (see e.g. Gasking, 1964). Thus, in uttering the sentence '$2 + 2 = 4$,' competent speakers are merely prescribing a metalinguistic norm:

> If two disjoint groups are counted such that '2' applies to each, then if one counts them together one should apply '4' to them.

Just as the moral nonfactualist denies that moral sentences express moral propositions, and hence represent putative moral facts, so the mathematical nonfactualist denies that mathematical sentences express mathematical propositions, and hence represent putative mathematical facts.

Notice that the mathematical nonfactualist, unlike the moral nonfactualist, is concerned less with mathematical predicates than with mathematical singular terms and quantifiers. The mathematical nonfactualist denies that competent speakers' use of mathematical language carries with it a commitment to the existence of mathematical objects, whereas the moral nonfactualist denies that competent speakers' use of moral language carries with it a commitment to the existence of moral properties. A fully general characterization of nonfactualism, then, one appropriate to the moral and mathematical cases, will have to abstract from the moral nonfactualist's specific semantic claims about predicates. The general idea in each of these cases is that the target sentences are not understood as expressing propositions that represent the putative subject matter. So, just as moral sentences are not understood as expressing distinctively moral propositions, mathematical sentences are not understood as expressing distinctively mathematical propositions. With this in mind, we can characterize nonfactualism, more generally, as the following claim:

Nonfactualism
The sentences in the target class do not express propositions that represent the putative subject matter.

As nonfactualism is an alternative to moral realism, the moral realist is committed to precisely what the nonfactualist denies: that moral sentences express moral propositions, and hence are representations of putative moral facts.

According to moral realism, however, it is not enough that the central commitments of morality be propositional and hence aspire to moral truth: they must also be true, or at least not wildly mistaken. Moral realism is thus opposed to the conviction that morality involves some fundamental mistake, some false presupposition about the contents of the world. John Mackie's (1977) error theory exemplifies this alternative to realism. Against the nonfactualist, Mackie contends that moral sentences express moral propositions, and hence are genuine representations of putative moral facts. Nevertheless, he believes that the facts they purport to represent are 'queer,' or would be if there were any, and best are not believed in. Mackie thinks that moral sentences purport to represent facts that are at once objective and essentially connected to the will—in the sense that forming a moral belief provides an individual with a motivation to act as a matter of necessity. But how could this be? If the moral order is objective, then it is independent of us. But if moral facts are independent of us, how could there be a necessary connection between what is right and what we ought to do? Our ordinary moral commitments involve a tension if not an outright contradiction—they seem to place inconsistent demands on what moral reality would have to be like in order for our moral beliefs to be true. Thus, Mackie believes that morality rests on a mistake, and that our moral acceptance and utterance involves us in widespread and systematic error.

The error theorist, like the moral realist, maintains that moral sentences express moral propositions. Moreover, the error theorist, like the moral realist, maintains that the acceptance of a moral sentence (in moral practice as it actually stands) involves belief in the moral proposition expressed. The error theorist, however, differs from the moral realist in further maintaining that we are in error in believing the moral propositions expressed by the moral sentences that we in fact accept, and hence we should not believe them. According to Mackie, moral properties are uninstantiated, and hence moral propositions are systematically false. But it is partly constitutive of belief that we should believe only true propositions. Insofar as the acceptance of a moral sentence involves belief in the moral proposition expressed, we should not accept the moral sentences that we in fact accept.

Notice that the error theorist claims that moral propositions are systematically false. He does not (or, at least, should not) claim that all moral propositions are false. Consider the proposition that lying is not right. According to the error theorist, the property of rightness is uninstantiated. So lying does not instantiate the property of rightness. So the proposition that lying is not right is true. So even the error theorist must admit that there are true moral propositions. Perhaps the error theorist should be understood as claiming that all *positive attributions* of moral properties are false. Unfortunately, there is no principled way of telling which predications are positive attributions. Consider the following:

X is mortal.
X is immortal.
X is not mortal.
X is not immortal.

Which of these predications are positive attributions and which are negative? There is no saying, and this undermines the thought that the error theory should be formulated in terms of the falsity of positive attributions of moral properties. To accommodate this complexity, I have characterized the error theorist's distinctive commitment as the systematic falsity of moral propositions. 'Systematic' is, admittedly, something of a weasel word in this context, but the obvious intent of the characterization should be clear.

Again, this species of irrealism is not peculiar to moral philosophy. There is an analogous position in the philosophy of mathematics. Field (1980, 1989) denies that there are any abstract objects—objects that do not participate in the causally integrated system of spatiotemporal events. However, Field believes that our mathematical theories express propositions that would commit one, if believed, to the existence of abstract objects—specifically, numbers, functions, and the like. Thus, according to Field, mathematical sentences express propositions that are systematically false. Not only is the error-theoretic alternative to realism not peculiar to moral philosophy, neither is it a peculiarly philosophical position. A more familiar form of error theory is atheism: the belief that the mistaken supposition that God exists discredits both theological discourse and the religious practice in which it is embedded.

The error theorist claims that moral propositions are systematically false and hence that we should not believe them. One might object that it is one thing to ascribe systematic error to the pattern of acceptance involved in actual moral practice and quite another to claim that we should not accept the moral claims that we in fact accept. After all, these claims are conceptually distinct. Moral acceptance might be moral belief, and such beliefs might be systematically false, but it might not follow that we should abandon those beliefs or suspend judgment concerning them. It is just barely conceivable that it is rationally permissible to continue to believe once we accept that error. Perhaps it is psychologically impossible for us to abandon our moral beliefs even in full recognition of the error they embody. Perhaps one can be an error theorist in the seminar room, but moral belief soon asserts itself when in the company of one's fellows—it might then be rationally permissible to continue to believe. Or perhaps the best thing to do is remain silent and try to forget, thereby ensuring that everyone continues to believe because of the disastrous social dislocation that would otherwise ensue. Just because moral belief involves some fundamental error, it might not follow that we ought to abandon moral belief once we accept that error: it might be rationally permissible to believe on the grounds of psychological impossibility, or on pragmatic grounds, or on some other grounds. But if that is the case, then it is not, after all, constitutive of belief, even in part, that we should believe only true propositions, and hence it is a mistake to say that the error theorist is committed to claiming that we should not believe moral propositions, because of their systematic falsity.

One could grant, if one were so inclined, that continuing to believe might be rationally permissible despite recognizing the error involved, but this is perfectly consistent with the view that belief is essentially truth-normed—that it is partly constitutive of belief that one should believe only true propositions. There are two ways in which this norm might be understood. It might be understood as a standard of criticism in terms of which beliefs are evaluated, or it might be understood as a guide to belief-fixation. As a standard of criticism, the norm is used to evaluate a belief. As a guide to belief-fixation, it determines whether it is rationally permissible for a person to adopt that belief. These two notions are closely related and can often coincide. An epistemic norm can at once be a standard of criticism and a guide to belief-fixation. Indeed, the way in which a belief may be positively evaluated might be grounds for adopting that belief. But the examples of the previous paragraph reveal that these notions can come apart. The claim that belief is essentially truth-normed should be understood as a claim about a standard of criticism partly constitutive of belief: it is part of the nature of belief that it is a state that can be positively evaluated as true or negatively evaluated as false. After all, there is something manifestly wrong with a false belief. But it doesn't follow from this that it is rationally permissible to believe only true propositions. The epistemic value of truth might be outweighed in a given circumstance by some nonepistemic value. In a context where serious social dislocation would ensue if the falsity of a moral doctrine were widely appreciated, the positive value of true belief might be an insufficient reason not to undergo an amnesia-inducing course of treatment. The objection to the norm of truth mistakes a standard of criticism essential to belief for a guide to belief fixation. If moral propositions are systematically false, one should not believe them according to a standard of evaluation partly constitutive of belief—whether or not one should believe them by some other standard relevant to guiding belief in the given circumstance.

The objection we have been considering began by distinguishing the claim that a range of beliefs are error-laden from the claim that one should abandon the beliefs recognized as error-laden. Given that an attribution of error does not entail that one should abandon the relevant belief, the objection continued, the error theory should be formulated in terms of the former and not the latter notion. Indeed, this argument, whatever its merits, is an argument for a standard formulation of the error theory. The error theory is standardly formulated in explicitly semantic terms:

> *Error Theory (Standard Formulation)*
> The sentences in the target class express propositions that represent the putative subject matter but are systematically false.

Given the standard formulation, not only must a realist regard the target sentences as expressing propositions that represent the intended subject matter, but he must also regard the propositions expressed by the accepted sentences as largely true (or at least not wildly mistaken).

However, there is independent reason to believe that the standard formulation is too narrow. Consider, for example, an agnostic about the existence of God. Such a person is, of course, no theological realist. He does not accept the central claims of theology. Indeed, he suspends judgment concerning them. However, it is also clear that the agnostic is not a theological nonfactualist—he believes that theological sentences express propositions that posit the existence of a deity. Indeed, agnosticism is a coherent epistemic stance only if a nonfactualist semantics is unavailable for theological discourse. The agnostic maintains that theological propositions are true only if God exists, but that the available evidence justifies neither the belief in God nor the denial that God exists. However, if theological sentences do not express propositions that represent a distinctively theological subject matter, then there is nothing for the agnostic to suspend judgment about, and hence no obstacle to his acceptance of them. Notice that both Mackie and the theological agnostic decline to believe the propositions expressed by the sentences that most competent speakers accept. It is their declining to believe propositions expressed by accepted sentences that is common to Mackie-style error theorists and agnostics. The error for Mackie is believing a false proposition, whereas the error for the agnostic is believing an unjustified proposition. If we are to make room for agnosticism in our taxonomy, then we should generalize the standard formulation of the error theory as follows:

> *Error Theory (Revised Formulation)*
> Competent speakers should not believe propositions expressed by the target sentences that they accept either because they are false or because they are unjustified.

As the error theory is an alternative to moral realism, the moral realist is committed to precisely what the error theorist denies: at least some of the central moral sentences that we accept express (at least approximately) true propositions that we are justified in believing.

On the standard conception of these issues, the conceptual terrain can be exhaustively represented as in Figure 1.

The Inadequacy of the Standard Conception

Unfortunately, the standard conception is inadequate or, at the very least, incomplete. It is a necessary condition for being a

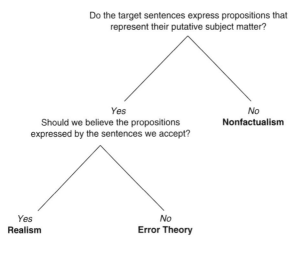

Do the target sentences express propositions that
represent their putative subject matter?

Yes
Should we believe the propositions
expressed by the sentences we accept?

No
Nonfactualism

Yes
Realism

No
Error Theory

Figure 1

moral realist that the acceptance of a moral sentence is belief in the moral proposition expressed. We have seen that, given the assumption that belief is a relation to a proposition, the moral nonfactualist's commitment to the nonrepresentation thesis precludes him from construing acceptance as belief in a moral proposition expressed. However, while nonfactualism implies this denial, the converse implications fail. Specifically, it is possible that moral sentences express moral propositions, and that the acceptance of a moral sentence is some attitude other than belief in the moral proposition expressed. To be a realist, then, not only must the target sentences express propositions that represent the intended subject matter, not only must they express true propositions that we are justified in accepting, but our acceptance of them must be belief about how things stand in the relevant domain.

While it is indeed a necessary condition on sentences purporting to represent the world that they express propositions and, hence, be truth-evaluable, it is not sufficient. It is not enough that the target sentences express propositions that represent the putative subject matter. Competent speakers who understand them must also put forward the target sentences as true—their utterance must normally assert the proposition expressed and their acceptance must be belief in that proposition. Contrast genuine assertions with the *faux* assertions of fictional discourse. In *Moby Dick* Melville writes:

It is not probable that this monomania in him took its instant rise at the precise time of his bodily dismemberment. Then, in darting at the monster, knife in hand, he had but given loose to a sudden, passionate, corporeal animosity; and when he received the stroke that tore him, he probably felt the agonizing bodily laceration, but nothing more. Yet, when by this collision forced to turn towards home, and for long months of days and weeks, Ahab and anguish lay stretched together in one hammock, rounding in mid winter that dreary, howling Patagonian Cape; then it was, that his torn body and gashed soul bled into one another; and so interfusing made him mad. (Melville, 1998: 165)

The passage describes the onslaught of Ahab's madness in the aftermath of his initial encounter with the White Whale. Whatever point there was to writing this, Melville is certainly not reporting the truth of some historical episode. The represented events have not transpired—a fact that is at least tacitly understood by both Melville and his reader. Melville literally asserts nothing about Ahab's madness, and the witting participants in the fiction literally believe nothing about Ahab. In a fictional context, the utterance or inscription of a sentence is not the assertion of the proposition expressed, and the acceptance of a sentence is not belief in the proposition expressed. Realism is thus opposed to fictionalism. Fictionalism is roughly the view that the target sentences, though they may express propositions that represent the putative subject matter, are, in fact, only representations that are somehow good or interesting or useful independently of their truth-value.

In the philosophy of science, van Fraassen's (1980) constructive empiricism exemplifies this alternative to realism. Constructive empiricism is usefully contrasted with operationalism. According to operationalism, the theoretical sentences of science do not express propositions that represent the unobservable structure of nature, but only the observable states of measuring devices. Thus, according to the operationalist, the meaning of the theoretical sentence 'There is a proton in the cloud chamber' does not involve reference to an unobservable entity, a proton; rather, it represents only that there is a vapor trail visible in the cloud chamber.

The constructive empiricist and the scientific realist are united in their opposition to operationalism—they each maintain that theoretical sentences express propositions that represent unobservable structures. However, the constructive empiricist maintains against the realist that the truth-value of a theory is irrelevant to its acceptability from the standpoint of science. The aim of science, according to constructive empiricism, is not truth but empirical adequacy—the representation of observable regularities. Scientific theories may posit the existence of unobservable entities, but an acceptable scientific theory may misrepresent unobservable matters of fact, so long as it is a reliable guide to observable phenomena. Thus, the constructive empiricist maintains that, even though the operationalist provides the wrong account of the meaning of theoretical sentences, he is nevertheless right in denying that the acceptance of a theoretical sentence involves belief in a theoretical proposition expressed.

According to constructive empiricism, then, the acceptance of a scientific theory is not belief in the theoretical proposition expressed. The constructive empiricist believes only that theory has a certain property, empirical adequacy. However, theory acceptance involves more than just the belief in its empirical adequacy. Acceptance has, as well, a significant practical component. Specifically, in accepting a scientific theory, the constructive empiricist intends to deploy that theory in the conduct of science, i.e. in experimental design, technological applications, the framing of explanations, and so on. Thus, according to constructive empiricism:

In accepting a theory T, competent speakers who understand T do not believe the theoretical proposition expressed. In accepting T, competent speakers believe only that the theory is empirically adequate and they intend to deploy that theory in the conduct of science.

Moreover, the epistemic policy of the constructive empiricist is reflected in his linguistic behavior. In seeming to assert a theory, the constructive empiricist merely asserts that it is empirically adequate and conveys his intention to deploy that theory in the conduct of science. In seeming to assert a theory that he declines to believe, the constructive empiricist is not being insincere. He is neither joking, nor lying, nor being sarcastic. This suggests that, in uttering a theory, he is not asserting the theoretical proposition expressed but is performing some distinct linguistic action.

To see this, consider the following. When a competent speaker utters a sentence, he normally asserts the proposition expressed. Moreover, in asserting a proposition, a competent speaker normally conveys to his audience that he believes the asserted proposition. If, however, it is evident, in the given circumstances, that the speaker does not in fact believe the proposition that he asserts, then he is susceptible to the charge of insincerity. Moreover, Searle (1969) has plausibly claimed that speech acts can be individuated by the attitude normally conveyed by their sincere performance. If Searle is right about the individuation of speech acts, then we can reason as follows. If an utterance is an assertion, then its sincere performance normally conveys belief in the proposition expressed. The sincere utterances of the constructive empiricist do not normally convey belief in the theoretical proposition expressed. Thus, the sincere utterances of the constructive empiricist must perform some linguistic action distinct from the assertion of the theoretical proposition expressed. Rosen (1990, 1992, 1993, 1994) has usefully described such linguistic actions as 'quasi-assertions.'

The theoretical utterances of the constructive empiricist are quasi-assertions, since they are not the assertion of the theoretical propositions expressed by the uttered sentences. There are two ways in which quasi-assertions can fail to be an assertion of the proposition expressed. Consider the following utterances:

Edgar likes the music of Ornette Coleman.

Does Edgar like the music of Ornette Coleman?

These utterances are distinct linguistic actions in the sense that they are distinct illocutionary acts. Whereas the former is an assertion, the latter is a question. Now consider the following utterances:

Edgar likes the music of Ornette Coleman.

Edgar dislikes the music of Wynton Marsalis.

These utterances are distinct linguistic actions, not in the sense that they are distinct illocutionary acts. Each is an assertion. Rather, these utterances are distinct linguistic actions in the sense that they assert distinct propositions. Whereas the former asserts the proposition that Edgar likes the music of Ornette Coleman, the latter asserts that Edgar dislikes the music of Wynton Marsalis. The quasi-assertoric utterances of the constructive empiricist can be distinct from the assertion of the theoretical propositions expressed, in two corresponding ways. A quasi-assertion might not be the assertion of a theoretical proposition either in the sense that it is an illocutionary act distinct from assertion; or in the sense that it is the assertion of some non-theoretical proposition. For present purposes, describing an utterance as a quasi-assertion is just the denial that it is the assertion of a proposition that represents the putative subject matter. Quasi-assertoric utterances might or might not be illocutionary acts distinct from assertion.

However quasi-assertion is to be understood, the epistemic policy endorsed by the constructive empiricist stands to sincere quasi-assertion as belief stands to sincere assertion. On the one hand, in sincerely asserting a theoretical sentence, the realist asserts the theoretical proposition expressed and so conveys his belief in that proposition; on the other hand, in sincerely quasi-asserting a theoretical sentence, the constructive empiricist merely asserts that it is empirically adequate and conveys his intention to deploy that theory in the conduct of science. In general, the fictionalist maintains that the sentences in the target class express propositions that represent the putative subject matter; but he maintains, as well, that their acceptance is not belief, and that their utterance is not assertion:

Fictionalism

The sentences in the target class express propositions that represent the putative subject matter. However, in accepting a sentence S in the target class, competent speakers who understand S do not believe the proposition expressed. Furthermore, in uttering S, competent speakers who understand S do not assert the proposition expressed; rather, they are performing the distinct linguistic action of quasi-assertion. Whereas sincere assertion normally conveys belief in the proposition expressed, sincere quasi-assertion does not.

Consideration of fictionalism clarifies the commitments of realism. Not only must the target sentences express propositions that represent the putative subject matter, not only must we be justified in accepting at least most of the target sentences that we in fact accept, but our acceptance of them must be belief in the propositions that they express. The conceptual terrain can be more accurately represented as in Figure 2.

Thus, three separable commitments are individually necessary and jointly sufficient for being a moral realist:

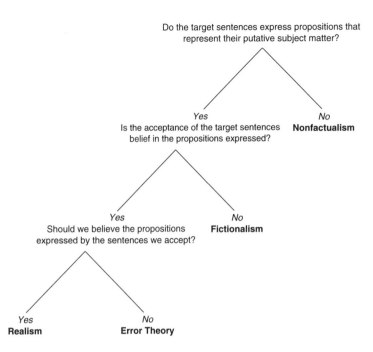

Do the target sentences express propositions that
represent their putative subject matter?

Yes
Is the acceptance of the target sentences
belief in the propositions expressed?

No
Nonfactualism

Yes
Should we believe the propositions
expressed by the sentences we accept?

No
Fictionalism

Yes
Realism

No
Error Theory

Figure 2

1. Moral sentences express moral propositions (propositions that attribute moral properties to things).
2. The acceptance of moral sentences is a belief in the moral propositions expressed.
3. Competent speakers are justified in accepting at least most of the moral sentences that they in fact accept.

One might object to the present taxonomy on the grounds that it leaves out one traditionally recognized form of moral irrealism. Many regard moral relativism, even a cognitivist moral relativism, as a form of irrealism. If moral relativism is a form of moral irrealism, then our taxonomy is incomplete and potentially misconceived. Correctly assessing this objection turns on locating the source of the intuition that moral relativism is a form of irrealism. According to the present framework, moral relativism is, instead, a form of moral realism coupled with a substantive claim about the nature of moral facts: There are moral facts—they are just relational. Compare the following. There are facts about motion—they are just relational facts. An object is in motion only relative to a spatiotemporal framework, and, the moral relativist maintains that an action is wrong only relative to a moral framework. The sense that moral relativism is not a form of moral realism is due to a substantive disagreement about the nature of moral facts. While moral realists agree about the existence of moral facts, they nevertheless disagree about their nature. Thus, moral realists have maintained that moral facts are facts about God's commands, human welfare, nonnatural states of affairs, and so on. The conviction that moral relativism is a form of moral irrealism is due entirely to a substantive disagreement about the nature of moral facts. According to the moral absolutist, moral facts, if there are any, are not relational the way the moral relativist claims them to be. According to moral absolutism, the most that could be claimed on behalf of moral relativism is that it correctly describes the facts actually tracked by our moral beliefs. From the absolutist perspective, if moral beliefs track only relational facts, then moral beliefs are systematically false. However, this is an error theory and is accommodated as such in the present framework.

Noncognitivism without Nonfactualism

Fictionalism is a kind of irrealism distinct from nonfactualism. Yet both the nonfactualist and the fictionalist accept the noncognitive thesis—the claim that the acceptance of a moral sentence consists wholly in attitudes other than belief in a moral proposition.

Consider the dilemma we faced at the end of the last chapter. We were impressed with the arguments for noncognitivism but were also impressed with the theoretical difficulties facing an expressivist nonfactualism. We appeared to be in the uncomfortable position of choosing between a plausible semantics wedded to an implausible cognitivism and an implausible semantics wedded a plausible noncognitivism. The apparent dilemma, however, is merely apparent—for a noncognitivist fictionalism eschews the semantics reckoned to be implausible. Fictionalism is noncognitivism without nonfactualism. Indeed, what distinguishes nonfactualism and fictionalism, on the one hand, from the error theory and realism, on the other, is precisely the cognitive status of acceptance. Whereas the nonfactualist and the fictionalist deny that acceptance is belief in a moral proposition, the error theorist and the realist maintain that it is (though they differ about whether such belief is justified). To designate nonfactualism as noncognitivism is to elide the difference between nonfactualism and fictionalism. Moreover, it is to presuppose illicitly that the nonrepresentational function of moral acceptance requires a nonrepresentational content for the accepted moral sentence.

The way out of our dilemma was anticipated by Alasdair MacIntyre:

Clearly. . . when one utters a moral judgment, such as 'This is right' or 'This is good', it does not mean the same as 'I approve of this; do so as well' or 'Hurrah for this!' or any of the other attempts at equivalence suggested by the emotive theorists; but even if the meaning of such sentences were quite other than emotive theorists supposed, it might be plausibly claimed, if the evidence was adequate, that in using such sentences to *say* whatever they mean, the agent was in fact *doing* nothing other than expressing his feelings or attitudes and attempting to influence the feelings and attitudes of others. (MacIntyre, 1981: 13–14)

MacIntyre observes that, even if emotivism provided the wrong account of the content of moral sentences, emotivism might still provide the right account of their use. Moral discourse may be fully representational—moral sentences may express propositions that attribute moral properties to things—but their acceptance might not be belief in a moral proposition but, rather, the adoption of the relevant emotional attitude; and their utterance might not assert a moral proposition, but convey only the relevant emotional attitude.

MacIntyre's suggestion that emotivism is a better theory of use can be understood as the expression of a fictionalist conviction. Whereas the significant distinction for the fictionalist about science is the distinction between the observable and the unobservable, the significant distinction for MacIntyre is the distinction between the normative and the descriptive. Just as the constructive empiricist claims that the totality of observable truths will not determine which theory to accept, MacIntyre claims that the totality of descriptive truths will not determine which moral sentences to accept (at least as moral practice is presently constituted). Moreover, just as the constructive empiricist claims that the truth about the unobservable is irrelevant to the acceptance of a scientific theory, so MacIntyre claims that the truth about the moral is irrelevant to the acceptance of a moral sentence in contemporary moral debate. In general, a fictionalist about morals maintains against the nonfactualist that moral sentences express moral propositions—they are genuine representations of putative moral facts. The fictionalist claims, however, that a competent speaker's acceptance of a moral sentence is not belief in the moral proposition expressed but rather some distinct attitude.

As our discussion of MacIntyre and emotivism suggests, a fictionalist could simply adopt an account of moral acceptance provided by standard noncognitivists. So, to consider one other example, perhaps Gibbard (1990) is right in claiming that moral claims are claims about the rationality of sentiment, and that in accepting a rationality ascription a competent speaker accepts a system of norms that permits the thing judged rational (where *norms* are something like prescriptions or imperatives).

A fictionalist could accept that claim about the nature of moral acceptance even if he rejected Gibbard's nonrepresentational semantics. The normative fictionalist maintains that normative discourse is representational—that normative sentences express normative propositions (propositions that attribute normative properties to things). The normative fictionalist denies, however, that the acceptance of a normative sentence is belief in the normative proposition expressed. Like the norm expressivist, the normative fictionalist maintains that the acceptance of a normative sentence is some attitude other than belief in a normative proposition, and that the utterance of a normative sentence is some linguistic action other than the assertion of a normative proposition. Indeed, the normative fictionalist can agree that the acceptance of a normative sentence is a state whose content can be represented by Gibbard's formalism (as he understands it) and that in uttering a normative sentence the content conveyed can be similarly represented. A normative fictionalist might even agree with Gibbard's explanation of normative acceptance and utterance as a biologically adaptive solution to a coordination problem. A normative fictionalist might agree that a speaker's acceptance and utterance of normative sentences can be explained without supposing that normative properties are instantiated, but that is consistent with the normative sentences expressing normative propositions nonetheless. Indeed, once it is appreciated that noncognitivism and nonfactualism are logically independent doctrines, the former being a claim about moral acceptance and the latter being a claim about moral semantics, it ought to be clear that a fictionalist could accept any of the accounts of moral acceptance provided by standard noncognitivists. If, however, the argument from aspect shift is sound, then moral acceptance is a certain kind of affect, a desire in the directed attention sense.

Most nonfactualists are noncognitivists not because of their nonrepresentational semantics. Typically, nonfactualists are noncognitivists on independent grounds. So, for example, some nonfactualists argue for noncognitivism on internalist grounds: they argue that moral acceptance is a motivating reason to act in a way that belief is not. Other nonfactualists argue for noncognitivism on epistemic grounds: they argue that moral acceptance is subject to disagreement in a way that belief is not. If sound, such arguments establish that moral acceptance is noncognitive. Indeed, nonrepresentational semantics were developed in order to accommodate the noncognitivism purportedly established by these arguments. This was a mistake. That noncognitivism about moral acceptance requires a nonrepresentational semantics is plausible only if one overlooks the fictionalist alternative. Since noncognitivism does not require moral discourse to be nonrepresentational, further argument would be required to establish nonfactualism. Thus, having established noncognitivism, moral fictionalism should be the default hypothesis, since the nonfactualist hypothesis involves further semantic commitments unnecessary to explain the noncognitive nature of moral acceptance. In a context where there is good reason to be a noncognitivist, fictionalism is a better hypothesis than nonfactualism, and not only because nonrepresentational semantics is unnecessary. Nonfactualism might not be a revision of moral language or even a partial revision— nonfactualism might purport to capture what we meant all along by our moral talk. However, if it does, moral language is misleading since it seems to be representational when in fact it is not. Moreover, as we have seen, expressivist nonfactualism faces serious difficulties. So in explaining the noncognitive nature of moral acceptance, the nonfactualist hypothesis involves not only unnecessary semantic commitments, but controversial ones as well.

According to moral fictionalism, moral sentences express moral propositions, but the acceptance of a moral sentence is not belief in the moral proposition expressed. This latter claim, the noncognitive thesis, might be described as *weak noncognitivism*: after all, moral acceptance might not be belief in a moral proposition and yet be belief nonetheless. *Strong noncognitivism* denies even this. According to strong noncognitivism, moral acceptance is not belief in a moral proposition, because moral acceptance is not belief at all:

Weak Noncognitivism
In accepting a moral sentence S, competent speakers who understand S do not believe a moral proposition.

Strong Noncognitivism
In accepting a moral sentence S, competent speakers who understand S do not believe any proposition.

Strong noncognitivism implies weak noncognitivism, but the converse implication fails: moral acceptance might not be belief in a moral proposition and yet be belief nonetheless. While weak noncognitivism is the important distinction from the perspective of distinguishing alternatives to realism, the standard arguments in the moral case for noncognitivism are arguments for strong noncognitivism. While the truth of fictionalism requires weak noncognitivism, it should be clear that fictionalism is consistent as well with strong noncognitivism. The standard arguments for noncognitivism might be arguments for strong noncognitivism, but even this stronger claim is consistent not only with nonfactualism, but with a semantically uncontroversial moral fictionalism as well.

Varieties of Quasi-Assertion

What is a quasi-assertion?

Initially, we have a negative answer: if the utterance of a sentence is a quasi-assertion, then it is not an assertion of the proposition expressed. How can we positively characterize quasi-assertions? There might be no unique answer to this question. The minimal negative characterization of quasi-assertion (as being distinct from the assertion of the proposition expressed) is what is essential, and there might be distinct ways in which this condition might be fulfilled in distinct regions of discourse. To have an idea of the options, it is useful to ask the following two questions:

1. What is the content of a quasi-assertion?
2. What are the conditions under which a sentence is quasi-assertible?

Let us begin with the first question. The difference between assertion and quasi-assertion is, at least in part, a difference in what is asserted. The content of the quasi-assertion is distinct from the proposition expressed. If an utterance is an assertion, then it normally asserts the proposition expressed. If, however, an utterance is a quasi-assertion, then it normally does not. Consider a disbeliever in astrology discussing the details of star signs with a believer. The disbeliever, in seemingly asserting that Mercury rising has an unsettling effect on a person's psychology, is not being dishonest or insincere. But if the disbeliever's sincere utterance does not convey belief in the proposition expressed, it is plausible to suppose that it is not the assertion of that proposition. But then what, if anything, does it assert?

Call the proposition expressed by a quasi-asserted sentence its fictional content. Call the proposition asserted by a quasi-asserted sentence, if any, its real content. Three views can be distinguished:

Metalinguistic Views
The real content of a quasi-assertion is metalinguistic: quasi-assertions are assertions about the content or some other property of a fiction.

Objectual Views
The real content of a quasi-assertion is objectual: quasi-assertions are assertions about real-world conditions related to the fictional content.

Nonassertion Views
While quasi-assertions have a fictional content, they lack a real content: quasi-assertions of sentences expressing propositions are assertions of no proposition.

Metalinguistic Views

On one interpretation of the disbeliever's utterances, when the disbeliever utters 'Mercury rising has an unsettling effect on a person's psychology,' he is making an assertion about the content of astrology: he is merely asserting that, according to astrology, Mercury rising has an unsettling effect on a person's psychology. Similarly, in the context of a discussion of *Moby Dick*, when a speaker utters 'Ahab went mad after his initial encounter with the White Whale,' he is plausibly making an assertion about the content of *Moby Dick*: he is merely asserting that, according to *Moby Dick*, Ahab went mad after his initial encounter with the White Whale. (See Lewis, 1978, for this approach to fictional truth.) Generalizing, one possible answer, then, is that the real content of a quasi-assertion is about the content of a fiction (where the relevant fiction can be an explicit fiction, a scientific theory, a moral doctrine, and so on). This has the consequence that:

The quasi-assertion of S is true iff according to the fiction F, S.

As long as a speaker is not independently committed to the truth of the fiction, then the quasi-assertion of S does not commit him to the truth of its fictional content. Thus, a moral fictionalist might claim that when, a speaker utters a moral sentence S, he is merely asserting that, according to prevailing moral standards, S. Similarly, the mathematical fictionalist might claim that, when a speaker utters a mathematical sentence S, he is merely asserting that, according to standard mathematics, S. (See Field, 1989, for this approach.)

Not all metalinguistic views maintain that the real content of a quasi-assertion concerns the content of a fiction. Some metalinguistic views maintain that the real content of a quasi-assertion concerns some other property of the relevant fiction. Thus, according to van Fraassen's (1980: 57) constructive empiricism, the utterance of a theory is not the assertion of its propositional content: rather, the speaker is merely 'displaying this theory, holding it up to view, as it were, and claiming certain virtues for it' such as empirical adequacy. As long as a theory can have these virtues independently of being true, the speaker is not committed to the truth of the theory. Another possible answer, then, is that the real content of a quasi-assertion is about some non-truth-involving property of a fiction. This has the consequence that:

The quasi-assertion of S is true iff S's fictional content has non-truth-involving property p.

As long as S's fictional content can have p independently of S's fictional content being true, the speaker is not committed to the truth of its fictional content. Thus, a moral fictionalist might claim that when a speaker utters a moral sentence S he is merely asserting that S's fictional content has the property that its acceptance would promote social utility. Similarly, the mathematical fictionalist might claim that when a speaker utters a mathematical sentence S he is merely asserting that S's fictional content has the property of being nominalistically adequate, i.e. correctly representing the world in all concrete respects. (See Balaguer, 1998, and Rosen, 2001, for different accounts of nominalistic adequacy.)

Objectual Views

The metalinguistic views discussed maintain that the real contents of quasi-assertions determine metalinguistic truth-conditions:

The quasi-assertion of S is true iff according to the fiction F, S.

The quasi-assertion of S is true iff S's fictional content has non-truth-involving property p.

Given that quasi-assertions involve the assertion of their real contents, these principles plausibly imply the corresponding principles governing quasi-assertibilty (i.e. principles that govern the conditions under which the claim is quasi-assertible):

S is quasi-assertible iff according to the fiction F, S.

S is quasi-assertible iff S's fictional content has non-truth-involving property p.

The converse implications fail, however. A fictionalist might accept either of these principles governing quasi-assertibilty but deny that the quasi-assertions have metalinguistic real contents. A fictionalist might claim that S is quasi-assertible iff, according to the fiction F, S but deny that its real content is about the content of a fiction. Such a fictionalist might maintain that the real content of S's quasi-assertion is about the real-world conditions that make it fictionally true that S. Similarly, a fictionalist might accept that S is quasi-assertible iff S's fictional content has non-truth-involving property p but deny that its real content is about p. Such a fictionalist might maintain that the real content of S's quasi-assertion is about the real-world conditions that make it the case that S's fictional content has p.

Let us begin with the first idea. It has two parts: first, that S is quasi-assertible iff according to the fiction F, S; second, that S has these quasi-assertibility conditions because its real content concerns the real-world conditions that make it fictionally true that S. How might that work?

Consider children playing a game of make believe. Suppose that Bernice and Edgar are playing Godzilla. That Bernice roars and approaches the sandbox menacingly makes it true in the game that Godzilla is attacking Tokyo. That Edgar leaps from the sandbox and makes swimming movements makes it true in the game that he is a refugee escaping via Tokyo Bay. Certain real-world conditions make various propositions true within the pretense. Walton (1990) calls the principles connecting real-world conditions with what is fictionally true the principles of generation.

The fact that fictional truths are systematically connected with real-world conditions via principles of generation can be exploited in a certain way. Utterances within a pretense make claims about what is true in that pretense. So in our example, if Edgar, seeing Bernice menacingly approaching, were to utter 'Godzilla is attacking Tokyo,' he would be making a correct claim about what is true within the pretense. But, given that the principles of generation connect Bernice's menacing approach with the fictional truth of Godzilla's attack, Edgar's utterance can be understood as asserting that the real-world conditions that make this claim fictionally true actually obtain. Thus, Edgar's utterance within the pretense of 'Godzilla is attacking Tokyo' can be understood as asserting that Bernice is approaching the sandbox menacingly. Another possible answer, then, is that the real content of a quasi-assertion is about the real-world conditions that make it fictionally true that S:

> The quasi-assertion of S is true iff real-world conditions c that would make it fictionally true that S actually obtain.

As long as a speaker is engaged in a pretense, then the quasi-assertion of S does not commit him to the truth of its fictional content. Bentham's (1932) suggestion that talk of rights is 'fictitious though not deceptious' might be developed along these lines. The idea is that competent speakers are implicitly engaged in a pretense according to which people have various rights. What makes it pretense-worthy that someone has a certain right is that he and others participate in a certain pattern of obligation. Thus, if a competent speaker were to utter 'x has a right to A,' he would, let us suppose, be making a correct claim about what is true within the pretense and thereby correctly assert that the relevant real-world conditions obtain, i.e. that a certain pattern of obligation obtains. Similarly, a mathematical fictionalist might claim that in making a mathematical utterance competent speakers are implicitly engaged in a pretense according to which the world contains, in addition to concrete objects, abstract mathematical objects. What makes it pretense-worthy that the number of moons of Jupiter $= 5$ is that there are five moons of Jupiter (a fact that can be expressed in the language of first-order logic without reference to the numbers). Thus, if a competent speaker were to utter 'The number of the moons of Jupiter $= 5$' he would be making a correct claim about what is true within the mathematical pretense and would thereby be asserting that the relevant real-world conditions obtain, i.e. that there are five moons of Jupiter. (See Yablo, 2001, for this approach to mathematical quasi-assertion.)

Let us consider the second idea. It has two parts: first, that S is quasi-assertible iff S's fictional content has non-truth-involving property p; second, that S has these quasi-assertibility conditions because its real content concerns the real-world conditions that would make it the case that S's fictional content has p. A version of constructive empiricism might be developed along these lines. The constructive empiricist might deny that the real contents of scientific quasi-assertions are metalinguistic. In quasi-asserting a theory a speaker is not asserting that it has certain virtues, among them empirical adequacy: rather, he is asserting that the conditions that make it the case that the theory would have these properties in fact obtain. So, for example, what makes it the case that a theory is empirically adequate is that the observable regularities are as that theory represents them to be. Thus, the quasi-assertion of the theory can be understood as asserting, in part, that the observable regularities are thus and so. Generalizing, another possible answer, then, is that the real content of a quasi-assertion is about the conditions that make it the case that S's fictional content has non-truth-involving property p:

The quasi-assertion of S is true iff real-world conditions c (which would make it the case that S's fictional content has the non-truth-involving property p) actually obtain.

As long as S's fictional content can have p independently of S's fictional content being true, the speaker is not committed to the truth of its fictional content. Thus, a moral fictionalist might claim that when a speaker utters a moral sentence he is merely asserting that the world is a certain way (i.e. the way it has to be to make it the case that its acceptance would promote social utility). Similarly, the mathematical fictionalist might claim that when a speaker utters a mathematical sentence he is merely asserting that the world is a certain way (i.e. the way it has to be to make it the case that the mathematical claim is nominalistically adequate).

Nonassertion Views

According to metalinguistic views, the real content of a quasi-assertion is metalinguistic: quasi-assertions are assertions about the content or some property of a fiction. According to objectual views, the real content of a quasi-assertion is objectual: quasi-assertions are assertions about real-world conditions related to the fictional content. On both views, quasi-assertions do not assert the proposition expressed (the fictional content), but they do assert some other proposition (the real content).

Another way for a quasi-assertion not to be an assertion of the fictional content is for it to be the assertion of no proposition. According to nonassertion views, while quasi-assertions have a fictional content, they lack a real content: quasi-assertions of sentences expressing propositions are assertions of no proposition. Davidson's (1984) account of metaphorical utterance is an instance of the nonassertion view. Davidson denies that a metaphorical utterance is the assertion of the proposition expressed, but he denies as well that it asserts any other proposition: it merely renders conversationally salient certain relevant dimensions of comparison. Thus, a moral fictionalist might claim that when a speaker utters a moral sentence he is asserting no proposition but merely conveying some noncognitive attitude. Similarly, the mathematical fictionalist might claim that when a speaker utters a mathematical sentence he is asserting no proposition but merely deploying a device to facilitate deductive proof. The linguistic reform of mathematical discourse implicit in Field (1980) might be an instance of this view. Field claims that mathematical utterances might be retained because of their deductive utility, but he declines to say what, if anything, they would be used to assert.

Acceptance stands to sincere quasi-assertion the way belief stands to sincere assertion. Thus, the structure of fictionalist accounts of acceptance should correspond to the structure of fictionalist accounts of quasi-assertion. We are now in a position to see that it does. Recall that the fictional content of a quasi-assertion is the proposition expressed by the uttered sentence and its real content is what is asserted, if anything. Three views about the real contents of quasi-assertions were distinguished. The real content of a quasi-assertion might be metalinguistic: quasi-assertions might be assertions about the content or some other property of a fiction. The real content of a quasi-assertion might be objectual: quasi-assertions might be assertions about real-world conditions related to the fictional content.

Quasi-assertions might not be assertions at all: quasi-assertions of sentences expressing propositions might be assertions of no proposition. On all three views, the utterance of the sentence is not the assertion of the proposition expressed. This latter claim, the nonassertion thesis, might be described as *weak nonassertion*. After all, as the metalinguistic and objectual views reveal, moral quasi-assertion might not be the assertion of a moral proposition and yet be assertion nonetheless. *Strong nonassertion* denies even this. According to strong nonassertion, moral quasi-assertion is not the assertion of a moral proposition because moral quasi-assertion is not assertion at all:

> *Weak Nonassertion*
> In uttering a moral sentence S, competent speakers who understand S do not assert a moral proposition.

> *Strong Nonassertion*
> In uttering a moral sentence S, competent speakers who understand S do not assert any proposition.

Strong nonassertion implies weak nonassertion but the converse implication fails: moral quasi-assertion might not be the assertion of a moral proposition and yet be assertion nonetheless. We have seen corresponding distinctions about moral acceptance. Just as moral quasi-assertion might be weakly or strongly nonassertoric, moral acceptance can be weakly or strongly noncognitive. Just as we can speak of the fictional and real content of a quasi-assertion, we can speak of the fictional and real content of acceptance. The fictional content of acceptance is the proposition expressed by the accepted sentence and its real content is what is believed if anything. Just as the real content of weakly nonassertoric quasi-assertion can be metalinguistic or objectual, so the real content of weakly noncognitive acceptance can be metalinguistic or objectual. And, just as strongly, nonassertoric quasi-assertion lacks a real content—no proposition is asserted; strongly noncognitive acceptance lacks a real content—no proposition is believed. Mixed cases are possible as well. According to the constructive empiricist, scientific acceptance is an amalgam of belief and intention, a fact that is reflected in linguistic usage. Thus, the structure of fictionalist accounts of acceptance corresponds to the structure of fictionalist accounts of quasi-assertion as required.

If the argument from aspect shift is sound, then not only is moral acceptance noncognitive, but it centrally involves a certain affect, a desire in the directed attention sense. While the fictional content of moral acceptance is the moral proposition expressed by the accepted moral sentence, its real content is plausibly limited to representing morally salient features of the circumstance. Not only does moral acceptance involve thoughts or perceptions about the morally salient features of the circumstance, but it also involves an appropriate affective response. This response consists in a tendency not only for certain features of the circumstance to become salient in perception, thought, and imagination, but also for these features to present a certain complex normative appearance. Moral acceptance not only involves thoughts or perceptions with real content, a proposition that represents the morally salient facts about the relevant circumstance, but also crucially involves a phenomenologically vivid sense of the moral reasons apparently available in the circumstance as the real content represents it to be. Thus, moral acceptance, according to the form of moral fictionalism argued for here, is a mixed case, involving as it does an amalgam of cognitive and noncognitive attitudes. However, if minimalism is correct, these attitudes are not distinct: the thoughts and perceptions involved in moral acceptance are events in a person's consciousness whose structure constitutes the relevant affect.

Circularity

Can a moral fictionalist provide an accurate noncircular specification of the attitude centrally involved in moral acceptance? Unfortunately, an accurate noncircular specification, while theoretically satisfying, might not be in the offing.

The noncognitivist claims that, in accepting a moral sentence, a competent speaker does not believe the moral proposition expressed, but, rather, expresses a noncognitive attitude. But what attitude is being expressed? A complete account of this kind needs to specify the relevant attitude, but one might legitimately doubt whether there is a noncircular way to specify these attitudes. According to Ayer (1946), in claiming that an action is wrong, a competent speaker conveys disapproval of it and provokes disapproval of it in others. But what kind of disapproval? Surely not aesthetic disapproval. If Ayer were to claim that what is being conveyed is moral disapproval, then circularity threatens. What, after all, is moral disapproval? While phenomenologically vivid, it is implausible to claim that moral disapproval has a distinctive phenomenal stringency that can individuate it from other forms of disapproval. Moral disapproval can be mild just as aesthetic disapproval can be severe. One natural way to understand moral disapproval is as the realist might: if a person morally disapproves of an action, he attributes to that action a moral property, such as wrongness, that merits disapproval of the action. Moral disapproval is understood as a response to an instance of wrongdoing. Since moral disapproval, so understood, presupposes beliefs about the wrongness of things, the noncognitivist cannot understand that attitude in that way. The fictionalist has the resources to provide an answer to the circularity problem. Or, rather, the fictionalist can make sense of the fact, if it is one, that there is no noncircular specification of the relevant attitude. Indeed, there are at least three ways in which a fictionalist might legitimately decline to noncircularly specify the relevant attitude.

The first way concerns the contingent expressive limitations of language.

It is well known that metaphors might have no complete paraphrase, especially ambitious metaphors such as 'Juliet is the sun.' While the fictional content of the metaphor can always be disquotationally specified, what is conveyed by the metaphor can at best be partially and approximately captured by paraphrase. Moreover, as Hills (1997) observes, such partial and approximate paraphrases are not always given in nonmetaphorical terms. Here is one such paraphrase offered by Stanley Cavell:

I understand by Romeo's words 'that Juliet is the warmth of his world; that his day begins with her; that only in her nourishment can he grow. And his declaration suggests that the moon, which other lovers use as an emblem of their love, is merely her reflected light, and dead in comparison; and so on.' (Cavell, 1969: 78–9)

The 'and so on' signals the partial and approximate nature of the paraphrase on offer. Notice as well that not one component of Cavell's paraphrase is given in nonmetaphorical terms. That Juliet is the warmth of his world is less a literal truth than a closely related metaphor that approximately captures but one aspect of Romeo's declaration. Similar remarks apply for every other component of Cavell's paraphrase. Juliet is not literally nourishment (Romeo has no cannibalistic intentions) and the moon does not literally reflect her light. For ambitious metaphors, there might be no nonmetaphorical way of specifying what is conveyed by the metaphorical utterance. Given the contingent limitations of language, metaphors may be expressively indispensable.

Similarly, if moral discourse is fictional, there might be no nonmoral way of specifying what is conveyed by a moral utterance. But why expect that there be in our language some alternative vocabulary for designating the relevant attitude? If there were not, this might be merely a contingent expressive limitation of our language rather than a principled objection to noncognitivism (a point easily missed if one assumes that God thinks in English and hence that everything real, being divinely ordained, is expressible in English). Of course a partial and approximate description of that attitude might be given. In accepting the wrongness of lying, an emotivist might claim that a competent speaker is expressing disapproval. Such a claim is only partial and approximate, since one might fairly wonder what kind of disapproval is being expressed (surely not aesthetic disapproval). There might be no nonmoral way of specifying the attitudes conveyed by moral utterance. Given the contingent limitations of language, moral vocabulary may be expressively indispensable in specifying the attitudes involved in moral acceptance. (Which is not to say that there would be no nonmoral way of specifying the relevant attitude in Enochian, the language of angels.)

Why expect that there be in our language the vocabulary for designating such an attitude (a contingent fact, if it is one) when moral vocabulary manages perfectly well to convey that attitude in ordinary conversational contexts? It would do no good to object that such an attitude would be mysterious. The fictionalist could reasonably retort that it is not at all mysterious but, rather, perfectly familiar—it is simply the attitude involved in moral acceptance and conveyed by our moral utterances. Indeed, the charge of mysteriousness is not a further objection but rather a reiteration of the circularity objection. For when pressed, the objector will doubtless point out that the relevant attitude is not any of the attitudes that we can describe in nonmoral vocabulary, so what on earth could the relevant attitude be? However, these are merely attitudes that we can describe in a contingently limited nonmoral vocabulary, and the relevant attitude is nothing other than the attitude conveyed by our moral utterances and involved in accepting uttered moral sentences.

The second way concerns the potentially parochial nature of moral acceptance.

Suppose noncognitivism is established by reflection on disagreements about reasons. That the disputants in a disagreement about reasons implicitly accept distinct principles that determine what would count as a reason for acceptance is a manifestation of their distinct moral sensibilities. The moral sensibilities of the parties differently structure the putative reasons available to them in a given circumstance—a fact that is manifest in a phenomenological difference between them. Given this difference in moral sensibility, the acceptance of distinct moral claims is plausibly the expression of distinct attitudes. There might, of course, be a parochial consensus about the nature of moral acceptance; that is, there might be local communities of judgment (see Gibbard, 1990: chapter 13) within which there is uniformity concerning the attitude that constitutes moral acceptance. However, such communities of judgment might display an imperfect uniformity, and a given individual might belong to several overlapping communities of judgment. Suppose, then, that moral acceptance is parochial in the following way: the acceptance of a moral claim consists in potentially distinct attitudes in distinct communities of judgment. Then there will be no general, substantive account of moral acceptance. Any such account would be elevating a potentially correct account of moral acceptance in a parochial setting to a false account of moral acceptance in general. Indeed, this is one of the mistakes that Nietzsche (1887/1989) attributes to the English psychologists. The English psychologists reason from the fact that moral claims are presently accepted by the English on the basis of their utility to the claim that in general moral claims are accepted on the basis of utility.

The third way concerns the role of normative appearance in desire in the directed attention sense.

Recall that a desire in the directed attention sense involves a tendency to focus on the object of desire as well as a tendency for the object of desire to have a certain normative appearance. So accurately specifying the relevant affect would involve specifying the object of the affect as well as the relevant normative appearance. If being subject to certain normative appearances is constitutive of having the relevant affect, then it ought not to be surprising that the best way to specify the relevant affect will involve the deployment of normative vocabulary. After all, how better to describe the relevant kind of appearance than in terms of what it is an appearance of? (If something appears red, how better to describe its appearance than as appearing *red*? There are, of course, alternatives, but these are invariably partial and approximate: 'It appears more like orange than yellow and not at all like green . . .') The best way to represent the relevant affect might be in terms of the normative properties apparently instantiated by the object of the affect. If that were right, and moral acceptance were desire in the directed attention sense, then no substantive account of moral acceptance would be possible—there would be no nonmoral way of specifying the attitude conveyed by moral utterance—but moral acceptance would be noncognitive nonetheless.

Suppose, then, that no noncircular specification were possible for the following reason. In order to specify the relevant affect one needs to specify the relevant moral appearance, and in order to specify the relevant moral appearance one needs to specify what it is an appearance of—the moral property apparently instantiated by some aspect of the person's circumstance. Conveying that attitude would involve conveying and so making public the relevant moral appearance. Representing some aspect of the circumstance as instantiating the relevant moral property would suffice to convey that appearance. But if the relevant moral appearance could not be specified except in terms of what it is an appearance of, then representing some aspect of the circumstance as instantiating the relevant moral property would be necessary as well. The represented moral property might be an essential objective correlative of the relevant affect. Noncognitivism does not require a nonrepresentational semantics, but if the relevant attitude is a desire in the directed attention sense, then noncognitivism might instead require a representational semantics. If that is right, then moral fictionalism might be the only available form of noncognitivism.

The realist is encouraged by the fact, if it is one, that the noncognitive attitudes involved in moral acceptance cannot be specified in nonmoral terms: in order accurately to specify the noncognitive attitude centrally involved in moral acceptance, one must represent it as a response to an instance of a moral property. The fictionalist concedes that an accurate specification of the relevant noncognitive attitude involves the representation of moral properties, but he denies that such representations are best understood as being put forward as true but claims, instead, that they have a noncognitive function.

So there are at least three ways in which a fictionalist might legitimately decline noncircularly to specify the relevant attitude: the first involves the contingent limitations of nonmoral language, the second concerns the potentially parochial nature of moral acceptance, and the third concerns the role of normative appearances in desire in the directed attention sense. Whereas the first and third ways are incompatible (if specifying the relevant affect involves specifying the constituent moral appearance, and this can be done only by specifying the moral property apparently instantiated, then a noncircular specification of moral acceptance is unavailable even in the language of angels); the second and third ways are not only compatible but mutually reinforcing as well.

Hermeneutic and Revolutionary Fictionalism

A fictionalist account of a given discourse can be understood in one of two ways. The fictionalist might be *describing* the discourse as it actually stands, or he might be *prescribing* that the discourse be reformed in a certain way. The fictionalist denial that acceptance is belief in a proposition that represents the putative subject matter might be a description of how acceptance functions in the target practice. Or the denial might be a prescription for reforming the acceptance of sentences in the target practice. To adapt the terminology of Burgess (1983), whereas *hermeneutic fictionalism* is a description of some actual discourse, *revolutionary fictionalism* is a prescription for reforming that discourse.

According to the argument from intransigence, moral acceptance must be noncognitive since the norms that actually govern the acceptance of a moral sentence differ from the norms appropriate to the cognition of the moral facts. Since the argument proceeds from a conceptual claim about the norms that actually govern moral acceptance, the resulting moral fictionalism is a hermeneutic moral fictionalism.

The fictionalist alternative to realism described in the previous section was a hermeneutic fictionalism. To see how revolutionary fictionalism fits into our taxonomy, first consider an error theory. When faced with the massive and fundamental error that the error theorist attributes to the target theory or discourse, a natural reaction is to reject that theory or discourse outright. This is the reaction of the most familiar form of atheist, for example. As the claims of theology come to nothing if God does not exist, we should simply abandon that intellectual endeavor. There is, however, a historically important variant of atheism that does not counsel the outright rejection of theological discourse and the religious practice in which it is embedded. The so-called freethinker believes that we should abandon our belief in God, but he does not thereby reject religious practice outright. For he believes that our theological commitments, while subject to massive error, nevertheless serve some important purpose. In particular, he feels that our theological commitments help maintain the social order. Instead of rejecting theological discourse outright, the freethinker believes it should be retained because it subserves some important instrumental purpose. A contemporary expression of the freethinker's stance is, perhaps, Tony Soprano's admonition to his son—'Even if God is dead, you're still going to kiss His ass.' It is clear from context that Soprano is motivated by a genuine concern for his son's well-being—he clearly believes that his son would be better off if he acted as if God existed despite his nonbelief.

The freethinker's position is both interesting and important. Too often philosophers treat religion as if it were nothing more than a primitive cosmological theory. The freethinker is commendable in emphasizing the noncognitive dimension of religious practice. Indeed, he considers it so important that he seeks to preserve it in the face of (what he takes to be) the error embodied in theological conviction. The freethinker is correct in recognizing that there is more to religious practice than the acceptance of a body of belief. (Compare: Erasmus' skepticism about rational theology was coupled with a defense of Christian piety.)

So there are two varieties of error theory depending on one's reaction to the discovery of some fundamental mistake. If, like the more familiar form of atheist, one rejects the theory or discourse outright, then one is an eliminativist. If, however, like the freethinker, one feels that the theory or discourse ought to be maintained because it serves some interest or purpose independently of its truth-value, then one is a revolutionary fictionalist. So understood, Mackie and Field are revolutionary fictionalists. Neither claims that we should reject or reinterpret our moral or mathematical discourse. Mackie does not believe that we should abandon moral discourse—indeed, after dispensing with the mistaken supposition that there are moral facts, he goes on to recommend various moral claims. Nor does Mackie reinterpret moral discourse. The moral claims that he advances are not invested with new meaning—a meaning free from the troublesome commitment to intrinsically prescriptive facts. (See Joyce, 2001, for an explicit development of a Mackie-style error theory as a form of revolutionary moral fictionalism.) Similarly, Field does not claim that we should abandon our scientific theories simply because of their commitment to abstracta. Nor does he reinterpret our scientific theories in nominalistically acceptable terms. Indeed, part of the attraction of Field's nominalism is that it avoids the difficulties facing nominalist reinterpretations of science.

Despite the error embodied in our moral and mathematical talk, each of these philosophers, respectively, holds that our moral and mathematical utterances do not have to be true to be good. Like the freethinker, Mackie believes that moral discourse should be retained because it is useful in maintaining social cooperation. And Field believes that, while science can be done without numbers, there is a practical advantage in formulating our scientific theories in terms of mathematical fictions.

The difference between hermeneutic fictionalism and revolutionary fictionalism concerns the attitudes involved in moral acceptance and pragmatics. For example, the constructive empiricist believes that, given the highest aspirations of our scientific endeavors, the acceptance of a scientific theory is best interpreted as some attitude other than belief, and that the utterance of a theory is best interpreted as a quasi-assertion. The freethinker's stance towards theological practice and discourse is markedly different. He maintains that the true believers genuinely assert God's existence and in so doing signal their belief. He is not, therefore, putting forward any interpretive or hermeneutic claim. Rather, he is recommending a revision in theological practice and discourse—the *cognoscenti* should not abandon theology *tout court*: rather, they should revise their attitudes to the theological sentences that they accept, and they should abandon assertion in favor of a species of quasi-assertion.

The difference between the hermeneutic fictionalist and the revolutionary fictionalist thus consists in an interpretive disagreement. The hermeneutic fictionalist maintains that it is a mistake to interpret acceptance as belief and utterance as assertion. Rather, reflection on the norms governing the acceptance and utterance of a sentence in the target class reveals that acceptance is some attitude other than belief in the proposition expressed and that its utterance is some linguistic action other than the assertion of the proposition expressed. The revolutionary fictionalist maintains that the acceptance of a sentence in the target class is belief in the proposition expressed and its utterance is normally assertion of that proposition, but he recommends a revision: we should revise our attitude to the propositions expressed by the sentences that we accept, and we should abandon assertion in favor of quasi-assertion. Fictionalism in our original taxonomy was a hermeneutic fictionalism. Thus, whereas MacIntyre maintains that reflection on the current state of moral disagreement reveals that our acceptance of moral sentences is some attitude other than belief in the propositions expressed, Mackie maintains that our acceptance of moral sentences is just belief in the propositions expressed; but given the error that they embody, we should revise our attitudes to the propositions expressed by the sentences that we accept. Moreover, whereas MacIntyre maintains that moral utterances are quasi-assertions, Mackie maintains that moral utterances are assertions; but given the error that they embody, we should effect a pragmatic revision and quasi-assert what we have hitherto asserted. While MacIntyre is making a sociological claim, Mackie is making a revisionary proposal.

Our diagram can be extended as shown in Figure 3.

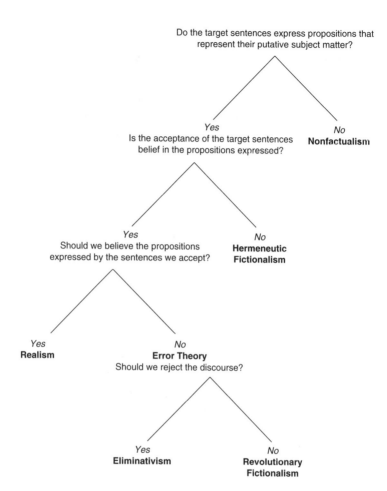

Do the target sentences express propositions that represent their putative subject matter?

Yes
Is the acceptance of the target sentences belief in the propositions expressed?

No
Nonfactualism

Yes
Should we believe the propositions expressed by the sentences we accept?

No
Hermeneutic Fictionalism

Yes
Realism

No
Error Theory
Should we reject the discourse?

Yes
Eliminativism

No
Revolutionary Fictionalism

Figure 3

There is a potential problem for hermeneutic moral fictionalism. According to hermeneutic moral fictionalism, actual moral practice is best described in fictionalist terms. Given the norms that actually govern moral acceptance, moral acceptance is best understood as some attitude other than belief in a moral proposition; and given the norms that actually govern moral utterance, moral utterance is best understood as some linguistic action other than assertion of a moral proposition. If, however, non-cognitivism is true, then moral discourse is systematically misleading, for moral discourse is apparently cognitive. The cognitive appearance of moral practice, however, raises a doubt about the hermeneutic ambitions of moral fictionalism. After all, the practitioners conceive of themselves as cognizing moral facts—they unhesitatingly ascribe moral beliefs to one another. If moral acceptance is noncognitive, then this self-conception is in error.

Hermeneutic moral fictionalism is indeed committed to a minor revisionism, and so, in this regard, there are limits to fictionalism's hermeneutic ambitions. But it is important to recognize what is being revised. Moral fictionalism is not necessarily committed to a revision of any of our distinctively moral commitments. Rather, moral fictionalism is committed to a revision of certain sophisticated epistemological beliefs about the nature of these commitments—that accepting a moral sentence is belief in the moral proposition expressed. Not only is the hermeneutic fictionalist committed to revising some of our epistemological beliefs, but he is committed as well to revising some of our linguistic beliefs. In making a moral utterance, competent speakers normally take themselves to be asserting the moral proposition expressed. But if hermeneutic moral fictionalism is true, then this is mistaken—competent speakers are merely quasi-asserting the claims of morality. According to the hermeneutic fictionalist, we might be justified in accepting most of the central moral claims that we in fact accept, at least by the standards of acceptability internal to moral practice; but we might nevertheless be wrong in describing our acceptance of these claims as moral belief and our utterance of them as moral assertion. However, notice that the claim that the acceptance of moral sentence is not belief in the moral proposition expressed is not itself a moral claim: rather, it is an epistemological claim about the nature of the attitude involved in accepting a moral claim. Similarly, the claim that the utterance of a moral sentence is not the assertion of the moral proposition expressed is not itself a moral claim: rather, it is a linguistic claim about the nature of the action performed by moral utterance. Competent speakers might be right to a large extent about the moral claims that they in fact accept, but they might systematically misunderstand what they are in fact doing when they accept and utter such claims. Since moral fictionalism is not necessarily committed to revising any of our distinctively moral commitments, the hermeneutic status of moral fictionalism is, at least to that extent, secure.

Moral Realism and Moral Epistemology

In the beginning of this chapter I remarked that it was unobvious what the commitments embodied in our use of moral language have to do with the metaphysics of morals. After all, the metaphysical commitments of a person as embodied in his use of language is one thing, and reality is quite another. I suggested that moral realism and its alternatives are better understood as epistemological postures or stances that are articulated in terms of the commitments involved in moral discourse. We are now in a better position to appreciate this point. I have argued that moral realism involves three components:

1. Moral sentences express moral propositions (propositions that attribute moral properties to things).
2. The acceptance of moral sentences is belief in the moral propositions expressed.
3. Competent speakers are justified in accepting at least some of the central moral sentences that they in fact accept.

Each of the alternatives to moral realism denies that we are justified in believing moral propositions expressed by the sentences we accept: either, as the nonfactualist claims, because there is no moral proposition to believe; or, as the fictionalist claims, because acceptance is some attitude other than belief in a moral proposition; or, as the error theorist claims, because such belief is unjustified. So understood, the alternatives to moral realism are kinds of moral skepticism in the minimal sense of denying that moral acceptance is justified moral belief. Thus, the nonfactualist is skeptical about the subject matter of morality, the fictionalist is skeptical about the cognitive status of moral acceptance, and the error theorist is skeptical about the justification of moral belief. Mistaking the philosophy of moral language for the metaphysics of morals obscures the way in which discussions of realism are covertly concerned with moral epistemology.

That is not to say that moral realism has no metaphysical commitments. The moral realist maintains that we are justified in believing some moral propositions, that we have reason to accept some moral propositions as true. But since truth is determined in part by extralinguistic reality, realism is committed to the existence of an extralinguistic moral reality. The epistemic stance of the moral realist commits him to the existence of moral facts. But a commitment to the existence of moral facts and the existence of moral facts are distinct states of affairs, the former epistemic and the latter metaphysical.

Our discussion of nonfactualism underscores this point. Strictly speaking, it does not make sense to speak of a nonfactualist metaphysics. Consider a hypothetical community whose moral discourse has a nonfactualist semantics. The existence of such a linguistic community is consistent with there being moral facts nonetheless. It is just that the members of this community would lack the linguistic means to represent these facts. This possibility, though abominable, seems perfectly coherent. This highlights the way in which moral realism and the irrealisms that oppose it are epistemic stances or postures. In the hypothetical situation just described, the community has, implicitly at least, succumbed to a mistaken skepticism about the subject matter of morality and has developed a moral language that reflects this skepticism.

Nor does it make sense to speak of a fictionalist metaphysics. Recall that the fictionalist about science does not make any substantive claims about the existence and nature of the unobservable portions of nature. Indeed, his acceptance of a theory consists neither in his belief that it correctly represents unobservable matters of fact nor in his belief that it misrepresents them. The only belief involved in accepting a theory is belief in the theory's empirical adequacy. Consider a hypothetical scientific community whose practice is broadly fictionalist. The members of this community accept only empirically adequate theories that they are disposed to quasi-assert. The existence of such a community is consistent with the unobservable structure of nature being exactly as the theories they accept represent them to be. It is just that, given the nature of moral acceptance, the members of this community would lack the means to know this. This possibility seems perfectly coherent. This highlights how fictionalism is an epistemic stance or posture. In the hypothetical situation just described, the community is skeptical about whether theory acceptance could be truth-normed and hence belief and has developed a scientific practice that reflects this skepticism.

The fundamental question for realism is whether we are justified in believing the moral propositions expressed by the sentences we accept. A failure to appreciate this point is manifest in the standard formulation of the error theory. As I remarked, the error theory is standardly formulated in explicitly semantic terms. Specifically, it is standardly understood as the claim that the target sentences express propositions that represent the intended subject matter but are systematically false. I have argued, however, that this characterization is too narrow, for it fails to include the agnostic. The agnostic does not claim that the propositions expressed by the target sentences are systematically false—indeed, he claims that we should suspend judgment concerning them. Both the atheist and the agnostic maintain that we should not believe the propositions expressed by the target sentences we accept. If agnosticism is included in our taxonomy of alternatives to realism, then the error theory should be understood as the claim that we should not believe the propositions expressed by the moral sentences that we accept, because they are false or unjustified. This reformulation, however, is explicitly epistemological.

The alternatives to moral realism are forms of moral skepticism because each denies that moral acceptance is justified belief in a moral proposition. They are not necessarily forms of skepticism in the further sense of claiming moral acceptance to be illegitimate or unjustified. Only the eliminativist claims that. In contrast, the nonfactualist and the hermeneutic and revolutionary fictionalists each claim that moral acceptance can be legitimate or justified—at least by the standards of acceptance internal to moral practice (as it actually is or as it might be reformed). This is an important qualification, for there is a distinction between acceptability by internal standards and genuine acceptability. The claim that Mercury rising has an unsettling effect on a person's psychology may be acceptable by the norms of acceptance internal to astrology, but it is not acceptable by the norms that many of us accept and regard as authoritative. The nonfactualist and the hermeneutic and revolutionary fictionalists might claim that we are justified, for the most part, in accepting the moral sentences that we do by the norms of acceptance internal to moral practice (as it actually is or as it might be reformed); but that is not yet to claim that they are genuinely acceptable. This raises the possibility that noncognitivism, whether in its nonfactualist or fictionalist guise, might be grounds for skepticism in the further sense of claiming that moral acceptance is illegitimate or unjustified. So consider the hypothetical community whose acceptance of moral sentences is governed by noncognitive norms despite the existence of moral facts. By the norms internal to their moral practice, a competent speaker may be justified in accepting a moral sentence because, let us suppose, he is justified in adopting the relevant noncognitive attitude. Nevertheless, the fact that moral acceptance is fixed independently of the moral facts is just grounds for criticism. Noncognitivism might be a correct description of the standards of acceptance internal to moral practice, but it is a further question whether moral acceptance, so understood, is legitimate or justified.

Conclusion

In Chapter 1, noncognitivism was urged on the basis of two arguments—those from intransigence and from aspect shift. In Chapter 2, however, we saw that the expressivist semantics involved in the standard development of noncognitivism faces serious difficulties in vindicating its nonfactualist and hence noncognitivist standing. If the arguments for noncognitivism are compelling, we faced a dilemma at this point: we appeared to be in the uncomfortable position of choosing between a plausible semantics wedded to an implausible cognitivism and an implausible semantics wedded to a plausible noncognitivism. The apparent dilemma, however, is merely apparent; for a noncognitivist fictionalism eschews the semantics reckoned to be implausible. If the difficulties facing an expressivist nonfactualism are indeed intractable, then an adequate noncognitivism requires the development of a semantically uncontroversial moral fictionalism.

4

Attitude, Affect, and Authority

Introduction

MORAL acceptance is noncognitive. Specifically, moral acceptance centrally involves a certain kind of affect, what Scanlon (1998) describes as a desire in the directed attention sense. In accepting a moral sentence that he understands, a competent speaker reconfigures his affective sensibility so as to render salient, in a phenomenologically vivid manner, the moral reasons apparently available in the circumstance, as he understands it. In accepting a moral sentence that he understands, a competent speaker quite literally decides how he feels about things. It is the structure of a person's moral consciousness and not some further fact that constitutes the relevant kind of affect. The relevant affect is nothing over and above the tendency for certain features of the circumstance to become salient in perception, thought, and imagination, and for these to present a certain complex normative appearance. Specifically, certain features of the circumstance become salient and appear to be reasons for acting, while other features potentially cease to be salient and can appear to be outweighed or even ruled out as reasons for doing otherwise, even if, in normal circumstances, they would count as such reasons. The salient features appear to be reasons that are not contingent upon our acceptance of them. Moreover, potentially distinct features of the circumstance become salient and appear to be reasons for accepting the moral sentence, and these reasons directly or indirectly involve grounding reasons, i.e. reasons that ground the deontic status of the relevant practical alternatives. These grounding reasons appear to be reasons not only for the speaker, but for everyone else as well. They appear to be sufficient for accepting that sentence on behalf of others. From this perspective, the competent speaker can seem justified in demanding that others accept the moral sentence and so come to respond affectively in the relevant manner. The affects centrally involved in moral acceptance are in this way essentially other regarding.

In uttering a moral sentence that he understands, a competent speaker conveys the relevant affect and implicitly demands that others come to respond affectively in the relevant manner. A moral utterance frames the perspective of its audience so as to induce the relevant affect. Notice that such framing effects are a hallmark of figurative language. Suppose that Bernice, in remarking about Edgar's *gravitas*, represents Edgar as a pear. Emma, in appreciating the aptness of Bernice's remark, cannot now but see Edgar as pear-shaped. Bernice's figure of speech has framed Emma's perspective so as to render salient, in a phenomenologically vivid manner, certain relevant dimensions of similarity between Edgar and pears. So, whereas the fictional content of Bernice's remark represents Edgar as a pear, its real content merely represents Edgar as pear-shaped. Moreover, the fictional content plays a role in this framing effect by focusing on the relevant features of the circumstance and by representing them in a certain qualitative light. So in accepting the aptness of this remark, Emma has a tendency to focus on certain features of the circumstance in perception, thought, and imagination, and a tendency for these features to have a certain qualitative appearance. Similarly, in accepting a moral sentence that he understands, the moral proposition expressed by the accepted sentence frames the perspective of the competent speaker so as to render salient, in a phenomenologically vivid manner, the moral reasons apparently available in the given circumstance as he understands it. So, whereas the fictional content of a moral utterance is the moral proposition expressed, its real content is plausibly limited to the morally salient features of the circumstance. Moreover, the fictional content plays a role in this framing effect by focusing on the relevant features of the circumstance and representing them in a certain normative light. So in accepting a moral sentence, a competent speaker has a tendency to focus on certain features of the circumstance in perception, thought, and imagination, and there is also a tendency for these features to have a certain complex normative appearance. The moral proposition expressed by the accepted moral sentence functions as an apt moral trope that frames the perspective of a virtuous moral sensibility.

A moral utterance conveys how a speaker feels about things. It does so not by virtue of an expressivist semantics that determines a nonfactualist interpretation for it. In reasoning from the non-representational function of moral utterance (in this instance, its framing effects) to the accepted moral sentence having a non-representational content, the expressivist plausibly conflates distinct senses of 'represent.' Moral discourse may be fully representational, moral sentences may express propositions that attribute moral properties to things, but the acceptance of a moral sentence might not be belief in the moral proposition expressed but, rather, the relevant kind of affect. Thus, for example, in accepting that the rights people have over their own persons ground the permissibility of abortion, Edgar has a tendency to focus on a certain feature of the circumstance, the embryo being essentially a part of the mother's body, and a tendency for this feature to have a certain normative appearance. In uttering this claim, Edgar conveys this affect and implicitly demands that others come to respond affectively in the relevant manner. Edgar conveys the relevant affect in part by conveying the relevant normative appearance. Moreover, Edgar conveys the relevant normative appearance by representing what it is an appearance of. In representing the embryo's being essentially part of the mother as the ground of her right to make an uncoerced decision to abort, Edgar makes public and so conveys the relevant normative appearance. The represented moral property is an objective correlative of the relevant affect. Moral propositions may constitute the fictional content of moral acceptance and utterance, but they do not constitute their real content (which is plausibly limited to representing the morally salient features of the given circumstance). Moral propositions, propositions that attribute moral properties to things, play a role in moral acceptance and utterance, not by being the objects of belief and assertion, but by being apt moral tropes that frame the perspective of a virtuous moral sensibility.

What makes it fictionally true that things instantiate moral properties? What makes an action good or just within the moral fiction? A schematic answer is available:

Suppose that moral predicate 'F' denotes moral property p. It is fictionally true that x is F iff x instantiates nonmoral property p^* that would elicit the relevant affective response in a person with a virtuous moral sensibility.

Since different attributions of moral properties differently structure the apparent reasons available in a given circumstance, we can be sure that different moral properties are paired with different affects. However, as we discussed in the previous chapter, there is no noncircular way to accurately specify the affect paired with the moral property. The affect is a desire in the directed attention sense, so accurately specifying that affect would involve accurately specifying the constituent normative appearance, and the only way of accurately specifying the constituent normative appearance is in terms of what it is an appearance of. However, the semantic indispensability of moral properties is no more problematic for a fictionalist interpretation of moral discourse than the semantic indispensability of metaphor is for a fictionalist interpretation of metaphorical discourse (see Hills, 1997, and Walton, 1993). Just as there is no noncircular way to accurately specify the relevant affective response, there is no noncircular way to accurately specify the kind of sensibility from which this response is elicited. It is the reasons apparently available from the perspective of a *virtuous* moral sensibility that constitute the relevant affect. (Different conceptions of moral virtue are possible and, if actually implemented in moral practice, would generate different and potentially competing moral fictions.) This is unobjectionable. Suppose that theology is a fiction. It would not be surprising that a range of affective responses were available only to the participants of a theological fiction—that it is only within the theological fiction that one could regard things as sacred or holy. Similarly, it should not be surprising that a range of affective responses are available only to the participants of a moral fiction—that it is only within the moral fiction that one could feel beneficent or just.

Within the moral fiction, there are facts about the existence and distribution of moral properties. Moreover, competent speakers accept sentences that attribute moral properties to things. It is natural, then, that within the moral fiction the acceptance of a moral sentence is belief about the attributed moral property—that it is fictionally true of a competent speaker that he believes the moral proposition expressed by the moral sentence he accepts. In accepting a moral sentence, a competent speaker does not so much believe the moral proposition expressed as he makes as if to believe that proposition, where making as if to believe, in this context, is to be disposed to respond affectively in the relevant manner. Acceptance in moral inquiry functions less to represent moral reality than to transform moral character by enabling competent speakers to respond affectively the way a virtuous person would. The aim of moral inquiry is not moral truth, but moral transformation.

Could We Discover that Morality was a Fiction?

What would be the rational response to the discovery that morality is a fiction?

There are both general and more specific questions here. The general question is: What would the rational response be to the discovery that morality is a fiction where at issue is the fictional status of morality and not the specific character of the moral fiction? A specific question is: What would the rational response be to the discovery that morality is a fiction if it had the character described in the previous section? Whatever the answer to that question is, the verdict might not be general. It might be the specific character of the moral fiction and not its fictional status that prompts the relevant response. In this chapter we will consider both questions.

This presupposes that we could, in fact, discover that morality is a fiction, but a doubt might be registered about this. Competent speakers unhesitantly describe their acceptance of a moral sentence S as believing that S. Could it really be the case that our attributions of moral belief are simply an unwitting pretense? So before we proceed, we will consider the prior question: Could we discover that morality is a fiction?

In Chapter 3 I argued that there were limits to the hermeneutic ambitions of moral fictionalism. While moral fictionalism is not necessarily committed to revising any of our distinctively moral commitments, it is committed to revising certain sophisticated epistemological and linguistic beliefs. In accepting a moral sentence, competent speakers take themselves to believe the moral proposition expressed; and in uttering a moral sentence, competent speakers take themselves to be asserting the moral proposition expressed. But if fictionalism is true, then competent speakers are systematically misconceiving what they are in fact doing when they accept and utter a moral sentence. According to hermeneutic moral fictionalism, moral acceptance is best understood as some attitude other than belief in a moral proposition, and moral utterance is best understood as some linguistic action other than the assertion of a moral proposition. We might be justified in accepting most of the central moral claims that we in fact accept, at least by the norms of acceptance internal to moral practice, but we might nevertheless be wrong in describing our acceptance of these claims as beliefs and our utterance of them as assertion. Notice, however, that the claim that the acceptance of a moral sentence is not belief in the moral proposition expressed is not itself a moral claim: rather, it is an epistemological claim about the nature of the attitude involved in accepting a moral claim. Similarly, the claim that the utterance of a moral sentence is not the assertion of the moral proposition expressed is not itself a moral claim: rather, it is a linguistic claim about the nature of the action performed by moral utterance. Competent speakers may be right about the moral claims that they in fact accept but may systematically misunderstand what they are in fact doing when they accept and utter such claims.

While hermeneutic moral fictionalism is not necessarily committed to any distinctively moral error, nevertheless, the fact that competent speakers so badly misconceive what they are in fact doing in accepting and uttering moral sentences might strike some as incredible. Don't we know what we are doing when we accept and utter moral sentences? (This objection is not confined to the special case of moral fictionalism. Indeed, Stanley, 2001, presses this objection against any form of hermeneutic fictionalism.) The challenge is to make it intelligible that competent speakers mistake what they are doing in accepting and uttering moral sentences without making the mistake impossible to discover. Indeed, there are several reasons why we might intelligibly be the unwitting participants of a moral fiction.

First, our attitudes and actions are not always fully transparent to us. Thus, it is plausible, for example, that a friend could be in a better position than you are to know that you are envious of a colleague and that a pattern of behavior that you have engaged in is an expression of that envy. Indeed, if your friend were to confront you and baldly assert that you are envious, you might initially deny it. However, if he were then to discuss the history of your relationship with your colleague and your behavior as seen from without, you might come, over time, to recognize what you initially denied. If this is indeed possible, then it is possible as well that an alien ethnographer could be in a better position than a native speaker to discover that in accepting moral sentences competent speakers do not believe the moral propositions expressed, and that in uttering moral sentences they are not asserting the propositions expressed. If the alien ethnographer were to confront a native speaker and baldly assert that his moral practice is fictionalist, the speaker might initially deny it. However, if the alien ethnographer were carefully to review the linguistic and ethnographic evidence with an open minded member of the linguistic community, such a speaker might come, over time, to believe that he was wrong all along about moral acceptance and utterance—that moral acceptance is not, in fact, belief in a moral proposition and moral utterance is not, in fact, the assertion of a moral proposition.

Second, one could not discover that morality was a fiction merely by reflecting on the content of moral vocabulary. Consider two possible worlds, w and w*. Both are near duplicates, the population of each speaks a moral language with identical moral vocabulary with the same representational content. However, in w, when a competent speaker accepts a moral sentence he believes the moral proposition expressed, and when he utters a moral sentence he asserts that proposition. In contrast, in w*, when a competent speaker accepts a moral sentences he does not believe the moral proposition expressed but adopts some other attitude, and when he utters a moral sentence he does not assert that proposition but performs the distinct linguistic action of quasi-assertion. If a speaker were to determine whether he was an inhabitant of w or w*, he could not do so merely by reflecting on the content of moral vocabulary. By hypothesis, moral content is invariant across w and w*. Semantic knowledge would not determine his location in modal space.

Third, it is not just that reflection on moral content would not reveal that morality was a fiction; in addition, reflection on moral content might tend to conceal that morality was a fiction if in fact it was. If, in reflecting on the contents of the moral sentences that he accepts, a competent speaker recognizes the representational nature of that content, he might naturally take himself to believe the propositions expressed and to be asserting them when making moral utterances. If moral content were representational, then in accepting and uttering moral sentences a competent speaker might naturally take himself to be representing the moral facts to himself and others. The speaker's mistake might be encouraged by the systematic ambiguity in our representational idiom. Sometimes by 'representing o as F' we mean that the proposition that o is F is being put forward as true. Sometimes by 'representing o as F' we mean that the proposition that o is F is expressed whether or not that proposition is being put forward as true. In the former sense a representation is being put forward as true; in the latter sense the content of a representation is being specified whether or not that representation is being put forward as true. However, if a speaker were unclear about the distinction, then he might mistake the purported representation of putative moral facts for the successful representation of such facts, and so mistake a noncognitive moral fiction for the cognition of the moral facts.

Moreover, there is a sense in which the cognitive appearance of moral discourse is both intelligible and predictable, given a fictionalist interpretation. After all, according to moral fictionalism, when a competent speaker accepts a moral sentence, he does not so much believe as makes as if to believe the moral proposition expressed. Making as if to believe, in this context, essentially involves adopting the relevant kind of affective response. Mistaking making as if to believe for belief is facilitated by the fact that attributions of moral belief are true within the moral fiction. The conditions that make a moral claim pretense-worthy for a competent speaker, if they obtain, also make the ascription of moral belief to that speaker pretense-worthy. That people believe the moral claims that they accept would be part of the extended moral fiction. Moreover, if attributions of moral belief are fictionally true, and moral pretense is unwitting, then it would be easy to mistake the fictional truth of such attributions for genuine truth, and so mistake a noncognitive moral fiction for the cognition of the moral facts.

What If Morality Were a Fiction?

Suppose we discovered that morality was a fiction. What would the rational response to the discovery be? Two observations are relevant here.

First, while a moral claim might be acceptable, given the norms internal to moral practice, nevertheless the acceptance of that claim might be illegitimate or unjustified by some relevant norm external to that practice. Compare: That Mercury rising has an unsettling effect on a person's psychology might be acceptable by the norms internal to astrology, but that does not mean that the claim is acceptable full stop. Suppose we reject astrology; then the claim is not acceptable given the norms external to astrology that we accept and regard as authoritative. So it is one thing for a claim to be acceptable by the norms internal to a practice and another for it to be genuinely acceptable from the perspective of our overall practice.

Second, in Chapter 3 I remarked that it was unobvious what the commitments embodied in our use of moral language have to do with the metaphysics of morals. After all, the metaphysical commitments of a person as embodied in his use of language is one thing, and reality quite another. I argued that moral realism and its alternatives are better understood as epistemological postures or stances that are articulated in terms of the commitments involved in moral discourse. This point is presently important because moral fictionalism is consistent with the existence of moral facts. A competent speaker's accepting a moral sentence might consist in a noncognitive attitude, but this is nonetheless perfectly consistent with the existence of moral facts.

These two observations combine in an obvious way. Suppose the norms governing moral acceptance were noncognitive. A moral claim might be acceptable by the norms internal to moral practice, but might not itself be acceptable because, let us suppose, it did not correctly represent the moral facts. Even though a moral claim is acceptable by the norms internal to moral practice, it might not be genuinely acceptable by norms appropriate to the cognition of the moral facts if indeed there were any. Moreover, if there were, then, while the acceptance of a moral claim might be justified by the norms internal to moral practice, the acceptance of that claim might be unjustified nonetheless.

This possibility, if actual, would constitute not only an epistemic difficulty, but a normative difficulty as well.

In accepting a moral sentence, a competent speaker accepts as well what reason is thereby provided. The reason involved in accepting a moral sentence (and conveyed in uttering that sentence) differs importantly from other reasons that the speaker might have. Moral reasons seem to have an authority that nonmoral reasons lack. While I did not give anything like a full account of the authority of morality in Chapter 1, I did describe the role it plays in moral discourse and in the cognitive psychology of competent speakers. One important feature of the authority of morality is the precedence that moral reasons take over nonmoral reasons. Specifically, in accepting a moral sentence, a competent speaker accepts as well a reason to act or to refrain from acting in a given circumstance that potentially overrides or cancels any conflicting nonmoral reasons available in that circumstance. So moral reasons differ from nonmoral reasons in that the former possesses an authority that the latter lacks—a fact that is manifest in the precedence that moral reasons take over nonmoral reasons. The authority of morality is manifest in other ways as well. Not only does a competent speaker, in accepting a moral sentence that he understands, accept a reason that takes precedence over nonmoral reasons, but he also accepts a reason that is not contingent upon his acceptance of it, for which there are grounds not only for him but for everyone to accept, where such grounds potentially justify demanding that others accept that sentence.

Suppose that, in accepting a moral sentence by the noncognitive norms of acceptance internal to moral practice, a competent speaker accepts as well a genuine reason. There nevertheless remains the question whether the accepted reason is a moral reason with the requisite authority. Suppose that a moral reason is a moral fact, or, at the very least, that the features of a given circumstance that count as a moral reason constitute a moral fact. Then in accepting a moral sentence by noncognitive standards of acceptance, a competent speaker would be mistaking a nonmoral reason for a moral reason. Indeed, he would be endowing the nonmoral reason involved in the acceptance of a moral sentence with the authority appropriate only to moral reasons. He would, for example, mistakenly treat the reason he accepts as having precedence over other reasons available in the given circumstance. Moreover, he would fail to recognize when the nonmoral reason that he accepts is overridden or cancelled by a competing moral reason available in the given circumstance. So not only would a competent speaker be misconceiving the nature of the reason that he accepts in accepting a moral claim, but he might be accepting no legitimate reason at all.

Morality in Plato's Cave

This is the situation that MacIntyre (1981: chapter 2) describes the Bloomsbury group as being in. According to MacIntyre, there was a radical discrepancy between meaning and use in the moral discourse of the Bloomsbury group. Given the meaning of moral vocabulary, the acceptance of a moral sentence seemed to involve the acceptance of a reason with the requisite authority. However, given the use of moral vocabulary, the acceptance of a moral sentence actually involved the acceptance of a nonmoral reason that lacked this authority. Specifically, their acceptance of a moral sentence was not governed by norms appropriate to the cognition of the moral proposition expressed (where the nature of the represented fact was the alleged ground of the authority of the accepted reason); rather, their acceptance of a moral sentence was governed by noncognitive norms. (For present purposes, what really happened in wci is irrelevant. What is presently important is that MacIntyre's account might be true, if not of the Bloomsbury group as they actually were, then of how they nearly might have been.)

According to G. E. Moore (1903), moral properties are nonnatural properties that can be intuited by persons with the appropriate moral sensibilities. Not only was Moore a nonnaturalist and an intuitionist, but he was a consequentialist as well: an action is right in a given circumstances just in case it produces more good consequences than any alternative action that is open in that circumstance. Moreover, Moore held a specific conception of the good: those things that instantiate nonnatural goodness to the greatest degree are personal intercourse and the beautiful.

According to MacIntyre, the Bloomsbury group embraced Moore's moral philosophy not on the strength of Moore's arguments, but rather because Moore's moral philosophy reflected the values they antecedently accepted. Their preferred form of life privileged the values of personal intercourse and the beautiful, just as Moore prescribed. Not only did the Bloomsbury group share Moore's conception of the good, but they were also disposed towards consequentialist forms of moral reasoning. Keynes reports that discussions of value involved the explicit ranking of states of affairs. He cites the following questions put forward for discussion:

If A was in love with B and believed that B reciprocated his feelings, whereas in fact B did not, but was in love with C, the state of affairs was certainly not as good as it would have been if A had been right, but was it worse or better than it would become if A discovered his mistake?

If A was in love with B under a misapprehension as to B's qualities, was this better or worse than A's not being in love at all? (MacIntyre, 1981: 16–17)

Moreover, such questions were resolved by appeal to intuition. The Bloomsbury group would focus on the target state of affairs and attempt to discern as best they could the presence and degree of nonnatural goodness instantiated in the target state of affairs. If there was disagreement, then either the disputants were focusing on different subject matters, or the moral sensibility of one was better placed to discern the presence and degree of nonnatural goodness than that of the other.

So it would seem that the moral practice of the Bloomsbury group was thus explicitly intuitionist—at least on the surface:

But, of course, as Keynes tells us, what was really happening was something quite other: 'In practice, victory was with those who could speak with the greatest appearance of clear, undoubting conviction and could best use the accents of infallibility' and Keynes goes on to describe the effectiveness of Moore's gasps of incredulity and head-shaking, or Strachey's grim silences and Lowes Dickenson's shrugs. (MacIntyre, 1981: 17)

If Keynes is to be believed, this is plainly the kind of manipulative noncognitivism for which Moore's student, Stevenson, has been criticized. On this view, the Bloomsbury group, in accepting an attribution of goodness, was not in fact tracking the presence and degree of nonnatural goodness. Rather, they were engaged in an unwitting pretense in which things have, in addition to their natural properties, certain nonnatural properties that supervene on them and that can be intuited by persons with the appropriate moral sensibilities.

Suppose that Edgar was a minor member of the Bloomsbury group. Being a faithful student of the *Principia*, Edgar understands the sentence

A's being in love with B under a misapprehension of B's qualities would be a better state of affairs than A's never being in love:

as Moore does—as representing a difference in the degree of nonnatural goodness instantiated by two potential states of affairs. Moreover, Edgar accepts this sentence. In what does Edgar's acceptance of this sentence consist? From within, Edgar's coming to accept this sentence occurred just as Moore describes: Edgar contemplates A's being in love under a misapprehension and A's never being in love and intuits that the former state of affairs instantiates nonnatural goodness to a degree greater than the latter. However, Edgar's intuition can be explained independently of the actual intuition of any nonnatural properties. Edgar accepts that A's being in love under a misapprehension is better than A's never being in love because, given his sensibility, Edgar approves of the former state of affairs more than he does the latter.

So there were two complementary principles governing this pretense. First, Moore's *Principia*, regardless of the truth of its doctrines, functioned as the master fiction of the moral pretense. In accepting and uttering moral sentences, the Bloomsbury group were acting as if the *Principia* doctrines correctly described the moral facts. If we confine our attention to attributions of nonnatural goodness, a rough statement of one principle governing the moral fiction would be:

> It is fictionally true that x instantiates nonnatural goodness iff according to the *Principia*, x instantiates nonnatural goodness.

Not only did the *Principia* prescribe, at least in general outline, which attributions of nonnatural goodness were fictionally true, it also prescribed an independent procedure for determining which individual attributions were fictionally true. According to the *Principia*, attributions of nonnatural goodness are accepted on the basis of intuition. What makes it fictionally true that a person is intuiting instances of nonnatural goodness is that, given their sensibility (a sensibility shaped by Moorean doctrine), they approve of that thing. Within the moral fiction, while nonnatural properties are distinct from natural properties, they nevertheless supervene on them. If a thing instantiates the (fictionally subvenient) natural properties, thereby endowing it with the tendency to elicit approval from persons with the appropriate sensibility, then it is fictionally true that it instantiates nonnatural goodness:

It is fictionally true that x instantiates nonnatural goodness iff x instantiates natural properties that would elicit the relevant emotional attitude in a person with the appropriate sensibility.

Putting these principles together, we get a principle connecting the emotional attitudes of the Bloomsbury group with the content of the *Principia*:

x instantiates natural properties that would elicit the relevant emotional attitude in a person with the appropriate sensibility iff according to the *Principia*, x instantiates nonnatural goodness.

In this way, the *Principia* both controlled and gave expression to the emotional attitudes of the Bloomsbury group.

But why did the Bloomsbury group express their amorous and aesthetic ends in the language of morality? Why this masquerade? MacIntyre suggests that, in rejecting the moral culture of the late nineteenth century in favor of a form of life that privileged the values of personal intercourse and the beautiful, what the Bloomsbury group lacked was a means justifying their preferences to others. Given the practical conflict between Victorian morality and their preferred form of life, the Bloomsbury group needed a means of rejecting at least those claims of Victorian morality that were incompatible with their ends; for, if the claims of Victorian morality were genuine, and so had the requisite authority, then, given the precedence of moral reasons, the reasons provided by these amorous and aesthetic ends were potentially overridden or even cancelled. In order to justify their rejection of Victorian morality and so pursue their preferred form of life, the Bloomsbury group needed to endow their ends with the authority of morality.

Moore's moral philosophy seemingly allowed them to do just that. The acceptance of Moore's moral philosophy was a means of reconceiving the nonmoral reasons provided by their preferences as moral reasons with the requisite authority. So doing seemingly allowed the Bloomsbury group to justify their form of life to their Victorian critics. Far from being at odds with morality, the privileging of the aesthetic and the amorous was precisely what morality required—at least from the perspective of the Moorean fiction that they accepted. However, insofar as these amorous and aesthetic ends provided reasons for acting in a given circumstance, what reason they actually provided lacked the authority of morality. Apparent instances of nonnatural goodness were merely shadows cast by amorous and aesthetic ends held independently of morality.

If moral practice were in this way fictionalist, then a cognitive reconstruction of moral practice would be required. We would need to turn from the shadows cast on the Platonic cave and look into the light: the noncognitive norms governing moral acceptance would need to be replaced by norms appropriate to the cognition of moral facts. Such a replacement would be not only epistemically required, but normatively required as well. The noncognitive norms governing moral acceptance would need to be replaced not only to justifiably believe the moral proposition expressed but also to justifiably act on the accepted moral sentence. The normative difficulty, after all, was that, in accepting moral sentences by noncognitive norms, competent speakers were accepting nonmoral reasons that were potentially overridden or cancelled in the given circumstance and so were potentially accepting no legitimate reasons at all. In the situation that MacIntyre describes, practical rationality requires justified moral belief, and a cognitive reconstruction of moral practice is needed before competent speakers can justifiably believe any moral proposition. Given the normative difficulty envisioned by MacIntyre, moral fictionalism, if accepted as a correct description of the way moral acceptance actually functions, would naturally lead to a revised and reconceived moral practice.

Benign Moral Fictionalism?

Moral fictionalism, however, is not necessarily committed to the normative difficulty envisioned by MacIntyre.

The difficulty with there being moral facts that moral acceptance fails to track is an instance of a more general difficulty. If there were moral facts and the acceptance of a moral sentence was at variance with the norms appropriate to their cognition, then in accepting a moral sentence a competent speaker would potentially be mistaking a nonmoral reason for acting in the given circumstance for a moral reason with the requisite authority. The more general difficulty is mistaking nonmoral reasons for moral reasons—reasons with the requisite authority. The authority of morality is manifest in the functional role that moral acceptance plays in moral discourse and in the cognitive psychology of competent speakers. Specifically, in accepting a moral sentence S that he understands, not only does a competent speaker accept a reason that takes precedence over nonmoral reasons, that is not contingent upon his acceptance of it, for which there is a grounds not only for him but for everyone to accept, but the competent speaker in uttering S demands that everyone accept S. Moral realists maintain that cognition of the moral facts best explains and renders intelligible the authoritative role that moral acceptance plays. However, moral authority need not be understood as the moral realist understands it. It is at least conceivable that, even if there were no moral facts, there would nevertheless be a legitimate distinction between reasons that possess the authority characteristic of morality and those that lack it. If this distinction can be made without commitment to the moral facts, and if in accepting a moral sentence competent speakers accept a moral reason, then a fictionalist moral practice need not be the kind of cultural disaster that MacIntyre describes.

Let us begin with the notion of a reason. Even if one denied that there were moral facts, one might nevertheless claim that there were facts about reasons. However, if one denied that there were moral facts one might deny as well that there were facts about reasons—perhaps the normative character of each presents similar obstacles to regarding both moral and normative discourse as being fully factual. Let us consider these options in turn.

Suppose there are no moral facts but there are facts about reasons. Nevertheless, a distinction might be drawn between moral and nonmoral reasons. Among the reasons that there are, some have the authority constitutive of being a moral reason. We typically convey moral reasons by means of moral utterance, but in so doing we are engaged in an act of quasi-assertion. We invoke a moral fiction in order to describe a particular kind of reason that is allegedly available in the given circumstance. Competent speakers convey that a feature of their circumstance has the normative significance that it does by invoking the metaphysical fiction of moral properties that supervene on those features and that ground their normative significance. So, while the fictional content of a moral utterance is a moral proposition, its real content represents a particular kind of reason—a reason with the requisite authority. There is a potential difficulty with this position, though perhaps not an insurmountable one. On the present view, there are facts about reasons and some of them are moral reasons. How is it that moral facts are not simply identified with the moral reasons? How are we to distinguish moral reasons from moral facts? If we cannot, then the present view collapses into a rationalist moral realism.

This difficulty might favor the second option. Suppose there are no moral facts and no facts about reasons either. Suppose, more specifically, that talk of reasons had a noncognitivist use, though not necessarily a nonfactualist one. How might this work? Recall Gibbard's (1990) strategy. Suppose that something's being a reason is understood as treating it as a reason. Suppose, moreover, that treating something as a reason is to accept a norm that prescribes that it count in favor of something. Then there will be norms corresponding to reasons, and whatever can be expressed in terms of reasons can be expressed in terms of norms. Suppose a competent speaker accepts that a feature of his circumstance is a reason to perform an action. While the fictional content of that claim involves the representation of a reason, it conveys the speaker's acceptance of a system of norms that requires treating that feature as counting in favor of the relevant action. Among the reasons, so understood, a distinction might be drawn between moral and nonmoral reasons.

So there are two ways to distinguish moral and nonmoral reasons while denying the existence of a distinctively moral range of fact. One might accept that there are facts about reasons and that some are distinctively moral, or one might deny not only that there are moral facts, but that there are facts about reasons as well (assigning, instead, a noncognitive use to our talk of reasons) and accept that some of the reasons that we recognize are distinctively moral. While the former option is a kind of weak noncognitivism, the latter option is a kind of strong noncognitivism. On the former option, a competent speaker in accepting a moral sentence accepts a moral reason where moral reasons are conceived as a kind of fact. While moral acceptance is not belief in a moral proposition, it is belief in a proposition that represents a kind of reason. On the latter option, a competent speaker in accepting a moral sentence accepts a moral reason where moral reasons are not conceived as a kind of fact. While moral acceptance is not belief in a moral proposition, neither is it belief in any other proposition. Mixed accounts are possible as well. Thus, on the present account, moral acceptance not only involves thoughts and perceptions that represent the morally salient facts about the relevant circumstance, but crucially involves a phenomenologically vivid sense of the moral reasons apparently available in the circumstance as it is understood to be. However, if minimalism is correct, these attitudes are not distinct: the thoughts and perceptions involved in moral acceptance are events in a person's consciousness whose structure constitutes the relevant affect. For present purposes, however, it does not matter which of these options are embraced so long as the denial of moral fact can be combined with the claim that some reasons are distinctively moral reasons and that these are the reasons involved in moral acceptance. As long as this distinction can be marked without postulating moral facts, and noncognitive moral acceptance involves the acceptance of moral reasons, then we can avoid the normative difficulty that MacIntyre envisions.

Attitude and Authority

Suppose that authoritative reasons can be operationally characterized in terms of the functional role they play in moral discourse and in the cognitive psychology of competent speakers. Perhaps a suitably complex yet coherently integrated system of noncognitive attitudes could implement that functional role in a way that would render intelligible why moral reasons would exhibit that role. Indeed, Blackburn (1998) and Gibbard (1990) each give accounts of roughly this form. Blackburn vividly expresses this approach as follows:

We should think in terms of a staircase of practical and emotional ascent. At the bottom are simple preferences, likes, and dislikes. More insistent is basic hostility to some kind of action or character or situation: a primitive aversion to it, or a disposition to be disgusted by it, or to hold it in contempt, or to be angered by it, or to avoid it. We can then ascend to reactions to such reactions. Suppose you become angry at someone's behaviour. I may become angry at you for being angry, and I may express this by saying that it is none of your business. Perhaps it was a private matter. At any rate, it is not a moral issue. Suppose on the other hand, I share your anger or feel 'at one' with you for so reacting. It may stop there, but I may also feel strongly disposed to encourage others to share the same anger. But then I am clearly treating the matter as one of public concern, something like a moral issue. I have come to regard the sentiment as legitimate. Going up another step, the sentiment may even be compulsory in my eyes, meaning that I become prepared to express hostility to those who do not themselves share it. Going up another level, I may also think that this hostility is compulsory, and be prepared to come into conflict with those who, while themselves concerned at what was done, tolerate those who do not care about it. I shall be regarding dissent as beyond the pale, unthinkable. This should all be seen as an ascending staircase, a spiral of emotional identifications and demands. The staircase gives us a scale between pure preference, on the one hand, and attitudes with all the flavor of ethical commitment, on the other. (Blackburn, 1998: 9)

Suppose that something's being a reason is a matter of treating it as a reason. Suppose, moreover, that treating something as a reason is to accept a norm that prescribes that it count in favor of something. Then, there will be norms corresponding to reasons, and it might seem that whatever can be expressed in terms of reasons can be expressed in terms of norms understood as non-cognitive attitudes. So instead of grounding reasons we might speak of higher-order attitudes. Suppose that, in accepting the wrongness of abortion, Bernice accepts a norm forbidding abortion if pregnant. Suppose, moreover, that she accepts higher-order norms that prescribe that she accept that norm, that everyone accept that norm whether or not they in fact accept it, and that she demand that others accept that norm. The authority of the demand might then be grounded in the higher-order attitudes that prescribe it. The general idea is that higher-order attitudes regulate which lower-order attitudes to accept and hence which features of the circumstance are to count as reasons. It is this regulative role in determining what counts as a reason that explains why the authority of the demand is grounded in the higher-order attitudes that prescribe it. Thus, the demand conveyed by Bernice's moral utterance would not be manipulative, and accommodating that demand could be a correction of attitude.

It is doubtful, however, whether higher-order attitudes could be the grounds of authority. There are three closely related grounds for doubt.

Suppose that Edgar accepts a higher-order norm prescribing that he accepts a norm prescribing guilt if he frustrates the expectations of others. Suppose, however, that Bernice expects Edgar to take the blame for her wrongdoing. Edgar may be socially obliging, but he is nobody's patsy: he is not disposed to feel guilty for not taking the blame. Indeed, he is not disposed to feel guilty, because he accepts a norm that forbids guilt in those circumstances. So Edgar accepts a higher-order norm that conflicts with a lower-order norm that he also accepts. How might this conflict between higher- and lower-order attitudes be resolved? Edgar might revise the lower-order norm forbidding guilt since it is inconsistent with a higher-order norm that he accepts. Indeed, this is part of the reason for thinking that higher-order attitudes could be the grounds of impersonal authority: the higher-order norms regulate which lower-order norms to accept and hence which features of the circumstance are to count as reasons. This is an illusion, however. Edgar might equally revise the higher-order norm. He may be obliging, and continue to be, but his confrontation with Bernice might reveal that obligingness has its limits, and he might revise his higher-order attitudes to reflect this. Everything else being equal, it is good when higher- and lower-order attitudes cohere, but when they conflict coherence can be achieved by revising either. But this undermines the idea that higher-order attitudes are authoritative: if higher-order attitudes regulate which lower-order attitudes to adopt, then coherence should be achieved only by revising lower-order attitudes but coherence may be achieved by revising higher-order attitudes as well. (Compare Watson's, 1975: 108–9, criticism of Frankfurt, 1971. Scanlon, 1998: 54–5, makes essentially the same criticism of desire models of reasons that appeal to higher-order desires.)

There is a second related ground for doubt. Higher-order attitudes differ from lower-order attitudes. Specifically, they differ in their objects: While higher-order attitudes have lower-order attitudes as objects, lower-order attitudes do not. But how could attitudes of fundamentally the same kind differ in authority when the only relevant difference is an intrinsic difference in object? If there was a puzzle about how certain lower-order attitudes could be authoritative all by themselves, it is hard to see how this puzzle could be resolved by appealing to attitudes of fundamentally the same kind that differ only in object. This difference in object could not ground the authority that the latter allegedly has over the former. The point is easier to appreciate if, instead of the higher-order attitudes that a person bears to his own attitudes, we consider the higher-order attitudes that he bears to the attitudes of others. Suppose that Bernice is angry at Edgar. Suppose that Edgar feels that Bernice's anger is unwarranted. He might be angry at her for being angry. In this emotional conflict, it is wrong to think that Edgar's anger is authoritative just because it has Bernice's attitude as an object—Edgar, after all, may be being unreasonable. Higher-order attitudes are higher-order not in the sense that lower-order attitudes answer to them, but only in the sense that they have lower-order attitudes as objects.

There is a third related ground for doubt. There are two ways to describe the case where Edgar revises the lower-order attitude incompatible with the higher-order attitude that he accepts: the case might be described as a mere change in attitude, or it might be described as a correction of attitude. Suppose that the higher-order norm is authoritative. Then revising the lower-order norm is not merely a change in attitude, but a correction of attitude. However, if, as the noncognitivist conceives of it, the conflict is between attitudes that cannot be jointly satisfied where the only relevant difference is an intrinsic difference in object, then there is no reason to think that the revision is anything other than a change in attitude. If the conflict were between accepting something as a reason for an attitude and accepting a reason that discounts that thing as a reason for that attitude, then the revision would be a correction of attitude. In the latter case, the relevant difference is not an intrinsic difference in object but a difference in the reasons for attitudes that intrinsically differ in object. The point is easier to appreciate if we consider the case where Edgar has all the relevant higher-order attitudes without regarding them as authoritative. Suppose that Edgar was raised to be socially obliging by domineering and psychologically adroit parents. Though Edgar cannot shake these attitudes, he can see no reason for acting on them. In these circumstances, if Edgar revises the lower-order attitude forbidding guilt, the revision would be a change of attitude and not a correction of attitude, since the revision is not a reflection of the reasons he accepts. Michael Smith describes a similar case in objecting to Blackburn (1998):

[W]e can readily imagine someone who (say) has a desire that people keep their promises, and who shares many other people's anger at those who fail to keep their promises, and who feels disposed to encourage others to share the same anger too, and who feels disposed to be angry at those who don't share that anger, and yet who doesn't regard any of these sentiments as being in the least legitimate. We need simply to imagine someone who, in addition, regards all his various attitudes towards promising in much the same way as the unwilling addict regards his addiction. He might think, for example, that these attitudes were all simply caused in him by social forces, in much the same way as the ingestion of drugs caused the unwilling addict's desire to take drugs in him, and that no reasons can therefore be given in support of acting on the basis of these attitudes, much as the addict thinks that no reason can be given for acting on his desire to take drugs. (Smith, 2001: 111–12)

Thus, in representing a correction of attitude in terms that could only represent a change in attitude, the noncognitivist fails to account for the authority of moral utterance. The demands they convey may be prescribed by a coherently integrated system of higher-order attitudes, but, nonetheless, such demands may be manipulative, and accommodating them might be a mere change of attitude.

It is doubtful whether noncognitivism, even in its fictionalist guise, could account for moral authority in terms of a coherently integrated system of higher-order attitudes. Even if no such account could succeed, perhaps the authority of morality could be vindicated in some other way by the noncognitivist. Nothing I have said so far has suggested otherwise.

A noncognitivist that maintains that moral acceptance is desire in the directed attention sense, and maintains as well a minimalist account of that attitude must—on independent grounds—provide another account of moral authority. Recall that desire in the directed attention sense can be characterized in terms of its functional role: in terms of the tendency for certain features of the circumstance to become salient in perception, thought, and imagination and the tendency for these features to present a certain normative appearance. The tendency for certain features of the circumstance to become salient and the tendency for these features to present a certain normative appearance would be both intelligible and well explained by the acceptance of norms that prescribe that these features have that normative significance. Thus, accounts of moral authority in terms of a coherently integrated system of higher-order attitudes would be the basis of an explanation for the functional role of the relevant affect. The minimalist, however, denies that desire in the directed attention sense is an attitude whose nature can be specified independently of its functional role, and that can explain and render intelligible why this attitude has that role. Given this, a noncognitivist that maintains that moral acceptance is desire in the directed attention sense and maintains as well a minimalist account of that attitude must account for moral authority in some other way.

Intransigence and Authority

Without speculating about how this might be done, let us consider a specific challenge to moral authority, given the present grounds for noncognitivism.

Recall that the argument from intransigence has three premises. First, public cognition is noncomplacent: if acceptance is cognitive and on behalf of others, then in the context of a disagreement about reasons, if a person is interested in accepting S on behalf of others, then he would thereby have a reason to re-examine the grounds of acceptance. Second, moral acceptance is authoritative: given its authority, moral acceptance is always acceptance on behalf of others. Third, moral acceptance is intransigent: in the context of a disagreement about reasons, a person interested in accepting S on behalf of others does not thereby have a reason to re-examine the grounds of moral acceptance.

To see how these claims constitute an argument for noncognitivism, first consider noncomplacency: if acceptance is cognitive and on behalf of others, then, in the context of a disagreement in reasons, if a person is interested in accepting S on behalf of others, he would have a reason to re-examine the grounds of acceptance. It follows that, if *moral* acceptance is cognitive and on behalf of others, then, in the context of a disagreement about reasons, if a person is interested in accepting a moral sentence on behalf of others, he would have a reason to re-examine the grounds of moral acceptance. This in turn entails that if, in the context of a disagreement about reasons, a person lacks a reason to re-examine the grounds of moral acceptance and moral acceptance is on behalf of others, then the moral acceptance is noncognitive. Notice that the antecedent of this conditional is just the conjunction of intransigence and authority. Moral acceptance is intransigent: in normal circumstances we are under no obligation to reexamine the foundations of moral claims that we accept, even if they are disputed by otherwise rational and reasonable, informed, and interested people who accept reasons that, if genuine, would undermine them. Moreover, given its authority, moral acceptance is acceptance on behalf of others. This could be so only if moral acceptance were noncognitive.

Even if a cognitivist were to resist this argument by denying intransigence, there would, nevertheless, be an important normative lesson to be learned. Being unmoved to further inquiry is subject to epistemic criticism since it violates norms appropriate to moral belief. The envisioned cognitivist would claim that being unmoved to further inquiry is subject to epistemic criticism because moral acceptance is cognitive, and if moral acceptance is cognitive, then, in the context of a disagreement about reasons, an interested person has a reason to inquire further into the grounds of moral acceptance. Not only is being unmoved to further inquiry subject to epistemic criticism, but it is subject to moral criticism as well. The claim that if moral acceptance is cognitive then, in the context of a disagreement about reasons, an interested person has a reason to inquire further into the grounds of moral acceptance is a consequence of noncomplacency and authority. So the noncomplacent character of moral acceptance is, in part, a manifestation of the authority of a cognitive moral practice. So from the cognitivist's perspective, being unmoved to further inquiry could only be a symptom of an underlying moral debility since the authority of morality would thereby be undermined.

Can an independent question be raised—one not involving any cognitivist assumptions—about the compatibility of intransigence and authority? Perhaps.

An interpretation of Kant's formula of humanity makes vivid the problem. Consider again Putnam's reaction to fundamental disagreement:

To be perfectly honest, there is in each of us something akin to *contempt*, not for the other's *mind*—for we each have the highest regard for each other's minds—nor for the other as a *person*—, for I have more respect for my colleague's honesty, integrity, kindness, etc., than I do for that of many people who agree with my 'liberal' political views—but for a certain complex of emotions and judgments in the other. (Putnam, 1981: 165)

What Putnam holds in something akin to contempt is Nozick's moral sensibility—a moral sensibility that privileges property rights over what Putnam regards as the compassionate treatment of the less well off. The question is whether something akin to contempt is the right attitude to adopt towards someone who in your view is lacking 'in a certain kind of sensitivity and perception.' Even if someone were lacking in this way, to treat him as an end is to treat him as capable, at least in principle, of acquiring the requisite sensitivity and perception. Moreover, to treat someone as an end is to allow for the possibility, however remote, that you yourself are lacking in this way. The difficulty of course is that contemptuousness is inconsistent with both these attitudes.

Treating someone as an end involves offering them reasons and treating them as capable of assessing those reasons. Conversely, it is to treat the reasons they offer as potentially genuine reasons that they are in a position to assess. It is this latter aspect of the formula of humanity that is presently relevant. What would it be, in the context of a disagreement about reasons, for Edgar to treat the reasons that Bernice offers as potentially genuine reasons that she is in a position to assess? It would involve, at a minimum, an openness to reflective doubt about his own grounds for the permissibility of abortion. This, in conjunction with an interest in accepting on behalf of others a claim about the moral status of abortion, is sufficient to motivate further inquiry into the grounds of moral acceptance. Edgar would have a motive to inquire further into the grounds of moral acceptance to determine whether, in light of his discussion with Bernice, his reasons for acceptance are good reasons. He would also have a motive to inquire further to determine, in light of his discussion with Bernice, what, if anything, there is to Bernice's reasons for rejection. Bernice, after all, might be onto something that so far eludes Edgar. Adopting the end of further inquiry is not only to strive to be responsive to what reasons there are, but to treat Bernice as an end and not merely as a means.

Of course, there is latitude in the fulfilment of this end. Further inquiry is one end among many and a person's ends must be rationally ordered—perhaps Edgar has more compelling immediate concerns. Particular actions taken to fulfil this end are epistemically meritorious, while particular failures to fulfil this end merely lack epistemic merit and are not in any way epistemically blameworthy (though perhaps adopting the policy of never acting to fulfil this end would be). There is an additional reason why adopting the end of further inquiry should display this normative structure. In this context, striving to be responsive to what reasons there are is to strive for moral perfection, to better respond to authoritative reasons. So, not only are actions taken to fulfil this end epistemically meritorious, but such actions are morally meritorious as well. Similarly, not only do particular failures to fulfil this end lack epistemic merit, such failures lack moral merit as well. Moreover, just as particular failures are not epistemically blameworthy, such failures are not morally blameworthy (though perhaps adopting the policy of never inquiring further would be). It is not surprising, then, that striving to be responsive authoritative reasons should display this normative structure, a normative structure plausibly assigned to perfectionist duties.

Edgar, of course, need not revise his moral opinion. Treating Bernice as an end need not involve Edgar's abandoning the claim that abortion is morally permissible, only that he be prepared to bracket his full acceptance of that claim when inquiring further. Nor need it involve a partial normative accommodation of Bernice's position—perhaps on due reflection her position on abortion has nothing to recommend. What it does require is that Edgar adopt the end of further inquiry. In this context, striving to be responsive to what reasons there are is a manifestation of moral virtue.

Intransigence is plausibly incompatible with moral authority. In the context of a disagreement about reasons, for Edgar to treat the reasons that Bernice offers as potentially genuine reasons that she is in a position to assess would involve, at a minimum, an openness to reflective doubt about his own grounds for the permissibility of abortion. This, in conjunction with Edgar's interest in accepting on behalf of others a claim about the moral status of abortion, would be sufficient reason to inquire further into the grounds of moral acceptance. Notice that the requirement that Edgar be open to reflective doubt is a normative and not an epistemic requirement—it is part of what it is, in this context, to treat Bernice as an end. Moreover, the plausibility of this normative requirement is independent of the cognitive status of moral acceptance. It merely presupposes that there are reasons for acceptance, but this would be plausible even if moral acceptance were noncognitive. So, given an interpretation of the formula of humanity, intransigence can be shown to be incompatible with moral authority without making any cognitivist assumptions.

If, according to the norms that govern moral acceptance, moral intransigence is intelligible, then such norms are subject to normative criticism. It is arguable that, under certain conditions, the apparent intelligibility of moral intransigence would fail to appropriately value the humanity of others. If that is right, then moral inquiry should be revised so as to become noncomplacent. The norms governing the acceptance of a moral sentence should be revised at least to the extent that, in the context of a disagreement about reasons, a competent speaker interested in the acceptability of S would be under a lax obligation to inquire further into the grounds of moral acceptance, at least if his disputant is otherwise rational and reasonable, informed, internally coherent, and similarly interested in the acceptability of S.

Renewed Moral Inquiry

In accepting a moral sentence that he understands, a competent speaker accepts as well what reason is thereby provided. Suppose a question is raised about the authority of these reasons given the norms that govern moral acceptance. Suppose, that is, that a questioned is raised about whether there are authoritative reasons that moral acceptance fails to track. Given the claims such reasons make on us, there would be reason to renew moral inquiry. Notice that the motivation is normative and not merely epistemic. If it were an open question whether there were authoritative reasons that moral acceptance fails to track, then moral inquiry, as it is actually conducted, would be potentially subject to normative criticism. There would thus be a normative and not merely epistemic reason to renew moral inquiry.

Moral fictionalism is consistent with the existence of the moral facts, and so it is logically possible that there are moral facts that moral acceptance fails to track. Moreover, if there were, there would be authoritative reasons that moral acceptance fails to track. However, this logical possibility is not sufficient to engender reflective doubt any more than the logical possibility that I am in the Matrix is. However, if moral intransigence were intelligible, then, as I have argued, a question could indeed be raised about whether there are authoritative reasons that moral acceptance fails to track. If, on whatever grounds, it were an open question whether moral acceptance tracks authoritative reasons, there would be reason to renew moral inquiry.

What form would such renewed moral inquiry take?

In order for renewed moral inquiry to be noncomplacent, it would need to be self-consciously conducted as a public inquiry. After all, it is partly for the sake of others that one should strive to be responsive to what reasons there are—that, in the context of a disagreement about reasons, one should adopt the end of further inquiry. It is nonaccidental that the results of such deliberation and, indeed, the deliberation itself can be presented in the medium of public language. Moral conversation, broadly conceived, is the proper medium of any such inquiry.

Renewed moral inquiry, so conceived, would not necessarily have as its aim the construction of a general and comprehensive moral theory. While a general and comprehensive theory for which there was noncollusive agreement among reasonable and rational people engaged in the joint endeavor of moral inquiry would be theoretically satisfying, it is unlikely to be achieved; nor should the aim of moral inquiry be anything so ambitious. The aim of renewed moral inquiry, rather, is to clarify our moral vocabulary and the grounds upon which we accept moral claims, to increase the coherence of the moral claims that we accept, and so on. This might result in a general and comprehensive theory, but then again it might not.

In clarifying moral vocabulary and the grounds on which we accept moral claims, and in increasing the overall coherence of our moral views, moral inquiry would rely on ordinary forms of public moral reasoning supplemented, where appropriate, by philosophical reflection. A philosophical theory of morality is by no means the grounds of moral inquiry. Rather, an adequate philosophical theory of morality would itself be grounded in the deliveries of moral inquiry.

As an illustration of this, consider the following: Suppose that renewed moral inquiry were undertaken not to redress the apparent intelligibility of moral intransigence, but to discover the moral facts if there are any. Having made a significant advance in the clarity and coherence of our moral views, even if large areas of disagreement remain, philosophical reflection on what has in fact been achieved might determine the cognitive status of that inquiry. In reflecting on the deliveries of the philosophically refined, public, moral reasoning we might be in a position to determine whether such reasoning was a form of moral cognition or whether the acceptance of moral claims on the basis of such reasoning remained noncognitive. In this way, a renewed moral inquiry might discover the moral facts if there are any.

If renewed moral inquiry essentially relies on ordinary forms of public moral reasoning, then what hope is there in its making any advance over actual moral debate? Two features of renewed moral inquiry are relevant here. First, moral inquiry is self-consciously conducted as a public inquiry—a cooperative venture whose end is acceptance on behalf of others. Moreover, it is a public inquiry that is motivated in a certain way. The point of engaging in renewed moral inquiry is for the participants in a moral fiction to assure themselves that there are not authoritative reasons that moral acceptance fails to track. This is an instance of what Rawls (1999: essay 22) has described as the burdens of reasons. The burdens of reasons are obstacles to a reasonable assessment of the moral reasons available in a given circumstance. The fact that moral acceptance is so burdened has normative implications for the conduct of moral discussion. After all, a fair-minded appreciation of the difficulties involved in assessing the authoritative reasons available in a given circumstance will affect how one interacts with others who disagree— even those who would disagree on fundamental matters. So renewed moral inquiry would be governed by reasonable precepts not only because it is a cooperative venture, but because of the motivation for embarking on that venture in the first place. That renewed moral inquiry is subject to the precepts of reasonableness is what distinguishes it from all too familiar forms of moral combat.

What are the precepts of reasonableness that are a reasonable response to the burdens of reasons?

Since it is a cooperative venture that aims at reasonable consensus insofar as that is possible within the moral domain, it should be conducted in a manner conducive to that aim. While disagreements may reasonably persist, there is no place for intransigence here. In the face of reasonable disagreement, allowing for the possibility, however remote, that one's grounds for accepting a claim are not decisive is not only a reasonable precept of cooperative inquiry but also a rational response to the burdens of reasons.

Not only should moral inquiry be conducted in a manner conducive to that aim, but basic disagreement should be reasonably accommodated as well. Suppose that reasonable people engaged in the joint endeavor of moral inquiry assess an action in a given circumstance by fundamentally different principles that practically conflict. One way in which such basic moral disagreement might be reasonably accommodated is to build a partial consensus on the basis of what can be agreed to. Working from this partial normative accommodation, the parties should try, insofar as possible, to understand what, if anything, the other is responding to. Persistent disagreements, even if basic, should be approached from a perspective that emphasizes what is undoubtedly a large measure of agreement. Doing so not only lessens the temptation to see the other as a moral monster but also provides a starting point for reasonable discussion.

As an example of this, consider how the abortion debate has changed. In the early stages of that debate, no defender of a woman's right to an abortion would concede that abortion was a bad thing, a fit object of regret even if justified. But that much is now conceded. Similarly, in the early stages of the debate, no prolifer would concede that abortion ought to be legally permitted even if morally forbidden. But that much is conceded, at least by many, no doubt in recognition that a decision to abort is a hard moral choice, combined with the conviction that people should make up their own minds about hard moral choices. This might suggest that the abortion debate has changed because the parties have partially accommodated the moral insights of one another. And this partial normative accommodation is plausibly a response to the reasons brought to bear by each side.

(I am unsure, however, whether this is the right account of the way in which the abortion debate has changed. The failure, early on, of the defender of abortion rights to concede publicly that an abortion is a fit object of regret might also plausibly be a rhetorical omission. Perhaps it was not conceded, not because it was rejected, but rather because to so concede would weaken the moral case for legalizing abortion. After all, it is hard to imagine a reasonably sensitive woman who actually had an abortion who did not at least concede the potential for legitimate regret, and so hard to believe that abortion being a fit object of regret was actually rejected. If that is right, then there was in fact no accommodation in this respect, and hence the change was not a response to the reasons brought to bear by prolife advocates. Similarly, the concession by many that abortion ought to be legally permitted even if morally forbidden might merely be the counsel of despair prompted by the realization that the state-sanctioned mass slaughter of the innocent is a permanent feature of modern society. If that is right, then there was in fact no accommodation in this respect, and hence the change was not a response to the reasons brought to bear by prochoice advocates. If this is the right account of the way in which the abortion debate has changed, then there was no tendency towards partial normative accommodation.)

These are not the only precepts of reasonableness. Rawls (1999) mentions, in addition, the reasonable expectation of disagreement and the crediting of one's interlocutor with good faith. There are undoubtedly others. I will not attempt to give anything like a comprehensive list, not least because such precepts should be determined, at least in part, from within the renewed moral inquiry. Just as other disciplines, whether psychophysics or econometrics, determine the methodology appropriate to their aim, so too should moral inquiry determine the methodology appropriate to its aim. So there is no saying in advance of such an inquiry what all of the precepts of reasonableness would be.

Moral inquiry here described is in some ways ideal. It is not ideal in the way that the Kingdom of Ends or Plato's Republic are; such an inquiry might be actually implemented in a way that the Kingdom of Ends or the Republic might not. Rather, it is ideal in that it is no substitute for practical deliberation. Due to inevitable practical exigencies, a decision to act or refrain from acting in a given circumstance might not wait on a consensus that may or may not emerge from moral inquiry. The participants of a renewed moral inquiry may have to act on moral reasons that they accept even if it is controversial whether such reasons have the authority that they take them to have. However, while moral inquiry is no substitute for practical deliberation, it is not entirely independent from it. Moral inquiry would depend, at least in part, on practical deliberation in that such deliberation is a potentially fruitful object of reflection for such an inquiry. However, just as importantly, practical deliberation would depend, at least in part, on moral inquiry in that the practical deliberation of the participants of such an inquiry would inevitably be informed by that inquiry. Moral inquiry would inform practical deliberation in at least two ways. First, moral inquiry would have the tendency to modify what one takes to be a morally relevant consideration in a given circumstance and so would affect how one would react to finding oneself in that circumstance. Second, the virtues involved in a renewed moral inquiry would naturally generalize beyond this initial setting. So, while moral inquiry is no substitute for practical deliberation, neither is it independent from it.

Conclusion

Renewed moral inquiry might have a number of outcomes. At one end of the spectrum, a revision of moral practice is both theoretically and practically required. At the other end of the spectrum, no such revision is required. But there are interim possibilities. Perhaps moral practice would remain fictionalist even after a renewed moral inquiry but the character of the fiction would change. Perhaps, while benign moral fictionalism is a legitimate possibility, the moral fiction that competent speakers actually accept is not itself benign. Or perhaps the actual moral fiction is in many ways benign but renewed moral inquiry suggests ways in which that fiction could be improved. There is no telling, in advance, what such an inquiry would reveal.

BIBLIOGRAPHY

Ayer, A. J. (1946). *Language, Truth and Logic*. London: Gollancz.

Balaguer, M. (1998). *Platonism and Anti-Platonism in Mathematics*. New York: Oxford University Press.

Bentham, J. (1932). *Bentham's Theory of Fictions*, ed. C. K. Ogden. New York: International Library of Psychology.

Blackburn, S. (1998). *Ruling Passions*. Cambridge: Cambridge University Press.

Burgess, J. (1983). 'Why I Am Not a Nominalist.' *Notre Dame Journal of Formal Logic*, 24: 93–105.

—— and Rosen, G. (1998). *A Subject with No Object*. Oxford: Oxford University Press.

Carnap, R. (1997). *The Philosophy of Logical Syntax*. Thommae Press.

Cavell, S. (1969). *Must We Mean What We Say?* Cambridge: Cambridge University Press.

Cohen, G. A. (2001). *If You are an Egalitarian, How Come You're So Rich?* Cambridge, Mass.: Harvard University Press.

Darwall, S., Gibbard, A. and Railton, P. (1992). 'Toward *Fin de Siècle* Ethics: Some Trends.' *Philosophical Review*, 101: 115–89.

Davidson, D. (1984). 'What Metaphors Mean.' In *Truth and Interpretation*. Oxford: Clarendon Press.

Dewey, J. (1945). 'Ethical Subject-Matter and Language.' *Journal of Philosophy*, 42: 701–12.

Eliot, T. S. (1932). 'Hamlet.' In his *Selected Essays*. London: Faber.

Field, H. (1980). *Science without Numbers*. Princeton: Princeton University Press.

—— (1989). *Realism, Mathematics and Modality*. Oxford: Basil Blackwell.

Frankfurt, H. (1971). 'Freedom of the Will and the Concept of a Person.' *Journal of Philosophy,* 68: 5–20.

—— (1988). *The Importance of What We Care About.* Cambridge: Cambridge University Press.

Gasking, D. A. T. (1964). 'Mathematics and the World.' In *Philosophy of Mathematics: Selected Readings,* 1st edn, ed. P. Benacerraf and H. Putnam. Cambridge: Cambridge University Press.

Geach, P. (1958). 'Imperative and Deontic Logic.' *Analysis,* 18: 49–56.

—— (1960). 'Ascriptivism.' *Philosophical Review,* 69: 221–5.

—— (1965). 'Assertion.' *Philosophical Review,* 74: 449–65.

Gibbard, A. (1990). *Wise Choices, Apt Feelings.* Cambridge, Mass.: Harvard University Press.

—— (1992). 'Reply to Blackburn, Carson, Hill and Railton.' *Philosophy and Phenomenological Research,* 72: 969–80.

Hare, R. M. (1952). *The Language of Morals.* Oxford: Oxford University Press.

Harman, G. (1977). *The Nature of Morality.* New York: Oxford University Press.

—— (1986). *A Change in View: Principles of Reasoning.* Cambridge, Mass.: MIT Press/Bradford Books.

—— and Thomson, J. (1996). *Moral Relativism and Moral Objectivity.* Oxford: Blackwell.

Hills, D. (1997). 'Aptness and Truth in Verbal Metaphor.' *Philosophical Topics,* 25(1): 117–53.

Hume, D. (1740/2003). *A Treatise of Human Nature,* ed. D. F. Norton and M. J. Norton. Oxford: Oxford University Press.

—— (1751/1988). *An Enquiry Concerning the Principles of Morals,* ed. J. B. Schneewind. Indianopolis, Ind.: Hackett.

Johnston, M. (2001). 'The Authority of Affect.' *Philosophy and Phenomenological Research,* 63(1): 181–214.

Joyce, R. (2001). *The Myth of Morality.* Cambridge: Cambridge University Press.

Kalderon, M. E. (2001). 'Reasoning and Representing.' *Philosophical Studies,* 105: 129–60.

Kant, I. (1785/1999). *Groundwork of The Metaphysics of Morals.* In *Practical Philosophy,* trans. and ed. M. J. Gregor. Cambridge: Cambridge University Press.

Kant, I. (1797/1999). *The Metaphysics of Morals.* In *Practical Philosophy,* trans. and ed. M. J. Gregor. Cambridge: Cambridge University Press.

Lewis, D. (1978). 'Truth in Fiction.' *American Philosophical Quarterly*, 15: 37–46.

—— (1983). 'Radical Interpretation.' *Philosophical Papers*, Vol. 1. Oxford: Oxford University Press.

McDowell, J. (1998). *Mind, Value, and Reality.* Cambridge, Mass.: Harvard University Press.

MacIntyre, A. (1981). *After Virtue.* South Bend, Ind.: Notre Dame University Press.

Mackie, J. (1977). *Ethics: Inventing Right and Wrong.* New York: Penguin.

Melville, H. (1998). *Moby Dick.* Oxford: Oxford University Press.

Moore, G. E. (1903). *Principia Ethica.* Cambridge: Cambridge University Press.

Musil, R. (1995). *The Man Without Qualities.* London: Picador/Macmillan.

Nagel, T. (1979). *Mortal Questions.* Cambridge: Cambridge University Press.

Nietzsche, F. (1887/1989). *The Genealogy of Morals*, trans. W. Kaufman. New York: Vintage Books.

Putnam, H. (1981). *Reason, Truth, and History.* Cambridge: Cambridge University Press.

Rawls, J. (1971). *A Theory of Justice.* Cambridge, Mass.: Belknap Press.

—— (1999). *Collected Papers.* Cambridge, Mass.: Harvard University Press.

Rosen, G. (1990). 'Modal Fictionalism.' *Mind*, 99: 327–54.

—— (1992). *Remarks on Modern Nominalism.* PhD dissertation, Princeton University.

—— (1993). 'A Problem for Fictionalism about Possible Worlds.' *Analysis*, 53: 71–81.

—— (1994). 'What is Constructive Empiricism?' *Philosophical Studies*, 74: 143–78.

—— (2001). 'Nominalism, Naturalism, Epistemic Relativism.' *Philosophical Perspectives*, 15: 69–91.

Ross, D. W. (1939). *Foundations of Ethics.* Oxford: Oxford University Press.

Scanlon, T. (1995). 'Moral Theory: Understanding and Diagreement', *Philosophy and Phenomenological Research*, 55(2): 343–56.

—— (1998). *What We Owe to Each Other.* Cambridge, Mass.: Belknap Press.

Searle, J. (1962). 'Meaning and Speech Acts.' *Philosophical Review*, 71: 423–32.

—— (1969). *Speech Acts: An Essay in the Philosophy of Language.* Cambridge: Cambridge University Press.

Smith, M. (2001). 'Some Not-Much-Discussed Problems for Non-Cognitivism in Ethics.' *Ratio*, 14(2): 93–115.

Stanley, J. (2001). 'Hermeneutic Fictionalism.' *Midwest Studies of Philosophy*, 25(1): 36–71.

Stevenson, C. L. (1937). 'The Emotive Meaning of Ethical Terms.' *Mind*, 46: 14–31.

—— (1944). *Ethics and Language*. New Haven: Yale University Press.

Strawson, P. (1950). 'Truth.' *Proceedings of the Aristotelian Society*, Suppl. Vol. 24.

Sturgeon, N. (1988). 'Moral Explanation.' In *Essays in Moral Realism*, ed. Geoff Sayre-McCord. Ithaca, NY: Cornell University Press.

van Fraassen, B. (1980). *The Scientific Image*. Oxford: Oxford University Press.

—— (1994). 'Gideon Rosen on Constructive Empiricism.' *Philosophical Studies*, 74: 179–92.

Walton, K. (1990). *Mimesis and Make Believe*. Cambridge, Mass.: Harvard University Press.

—— (1993). 'Metaphor and Prop-Oriented Make-Believe.' *European Journal of Philosophy*, 1: 39–57.

Watson, G. (1975). 'Free Agency.' *Journal of Philosophy*, 72: 205–20.

Wedgwood, R. (2001). 'Conceptual Role Semantics for Moral Terms.' *Philosophical Review*, 110: 1–30.

Wittgenstein, L. (1958). *The Philosophical Investigations*. New York: Macmillan.

Yablo, S. (2000). 'Apriority and Existence.' In *New Essays on the Apriori*, ed. by P. Boghossian and C. Peacocke. Oxford: Oxford University Press.

—— (2001). 'Go Figure: A Path through Fictionalism.' *Midwest Studies in Philosophy* 25(1): 72–102.

INDEX